St George In My Heart

confessions of an England fan

Colin Johnson

A TERRACE BANTER PUBLICATION

*To all the chaps who have taken the trouble to defy
the authorities and make their own way across land and sea
to follow England away. No surrender!*

St George In My Heart - Confessions Of An England Fan (Pbk)

© Colin Johnson, 2000

ISBN 0 9535920 3 0

Published by Terrace Banter, Scotland
Printed by Heritage Press & Publishing, England

From cover photo: Italy versus England, 1997
Back cover photo: Holland versus England, 1993

A Terrace Banter publication from
S.T. Publishing
P.O. Box 12, Lockerbie, Dumfriesshire. DG11 3BW. Scotland.

www.terracebanter.com   info@terracebanter.com

St George In My Heart

confessions of an England fan

Welcome to England

ALTHOUGH I HAD been regularly going to Millwall for a
few years, I had only become interested in following
England away in the Autumn of 1987. England had
qualified for the European Championships to be played in
Germany the following summer, and in an effort to
prepare themselves for the invasion of thousands of
young, aggressive Englishmen, the German authorities
had come up with the madcap idea of playing a friendly
against England in Düsseldorf.

For many people, there could be no such thing as a friendly
between the two nations at any sport, let alone football. There was
plenty of drunken chat in my local pub about us going to Düsseldorf
for the game despite the fact that most of us were just 16 and had
only recently left school. Although the idea appealed to me, I had
always regarded the behaviour of the England away fans as mental.
I had been involved in trouble at Millwall, but I was always one of the
many kids who just made up the numbers. I charged when the big
boys charged, and I ran for my life if it started to look like it might get
on top. And I knew that if you went abroad with England, you were
playing for higher stakes. You risked your personal safety, being
deported and plastered all over the papers, and the most frightening
thing of all - doing bird in a foreign nick. I was wise enough even at
sweet 16 to give Germany a miss.

One of my mates, Andy, had declared his intention of going so
forthrightly, that he now had to go otherwise he would start to look
like a bit of a clown. He used to go to Chelsea and had become
friendly with a few of their boys, and rumour had it that they had
organised a coach trip to Germany. He told us that these boys had
told him to turn up in Wandsworth on the Monday before the game,
and although the coach was supposed to be fully booked up, he was
told that if anyone was to drop out he could take the spare seat.

On the day of the game, I still hadn't heard from Andy and
assumed that he had made it to Germany. News of the clashes
between the rival fans in the Altstadt dominated the newspapers and
I scanned every page looking for Andy. I had always been

interested in what the English supporters got up to on these trips, but on this occasion I became obsessed about what was going on because one of my mates was actually there.

Anyway, I never found Andy in any of the papers, and was gutted when he phoned me up the following day and said that he hadn't even got as far as Wandsworth. Nonetheless, the possibility of one of my mates being there had ignited a strange feeling inside me, but I still didn't feel quite ready to make the transition from teenage groupie at Millwall to game for anything England hooligan, ready to mix it with some of the main boys from clubs throughout the country, in hostile countries far from home.

In March, 1988, England had arranged to play Holland in a friendly at Wembley. We were due to play Holland in the group stages of the Championships, so in many ways this was a warm up to the vital game to come later that summer. For quite a few years, the problem of football related disorder had been creeping into the Dutch domestic game and teams like Ajax, Feyenoord and Den Haag all had significant reputations for being able to attract large numbers of hooligans. Weapons such as knives and C.S. gas canisters are much more widely available on the Continent than in England, and it was reported that many of the skirmishes between the Dutch fans involved such weapons.

The English media, as usual, built up the game to be a battle for the number one spot in the prestigious European hooligan leagues that were continually being published at the time. Apparently, the Dutch were in top spot, with the English in third place behind them and the Germans. There were numerous interviews with 'top boy' hooligans from Holland, boasting about how they were coming to London to wreck our capital city. The media like to portray themselves as anti-violence, but irresponsible journalism such as this can only increase the potential for trouble. It really is quite ironic that after violence erupts at games like this, journalists behave as if they are holier than thou and make hysterical calls for the fans to be arrested and caged for life. Many of the tabloid hacks need football violence to justify their own trips abroad. Much of their time following England is spent in seedy bars and brothels, large sums are made on fraudulent expense claims, and on more than one occasion they have even paid some gullible English fans to start trouble to make their job even easier.

It soon became apparent that every firm in the country would be converging on London to do battle with their Dutch counterparts before, during, and after the game. And as it turned out, about 15 of us made the short journey into London. As we crossed into North London, firms from all over the country boarded the tube at various stations. By the time we arrived at Wembley Park, the tube was packed with hundreds of young English hooligans, ready for action. There were however no Dutch fans to be seen.

Most of the boys on the tube did not have tickets for the game which was already a sell-out. No one seemed concerned at the possibility of missing Ruud Gullit and Marco Van Basten in action. There were plenty of touts outside the station, offering tickets for sale at extortionate prices, but no one was really making any effort to obtain a match ticket.

Wembley Way was packed with fans. However, these were not the type of supporters Sky TV are now so fond of showing in the build up to games at Wembley. Everyone here was part of a mob. There were 30 or so Derby fans, a mob of Boro fans, a particularly mean looking group of Bolton fans, and a huge mob of Birmingham. Obviously, all the large London firms were there as well. These mobs had been fighting each other every Saturday for years and years, but on this particular night, all the old rivalries were to be temporarily laid to rest. Well, almost.

Up near the stadium, we were all loitering around. The police wanted us off the streets, for obvious reasons, but as most of us were ticketless, we could not enter the stadium. There seemed to be a tense stand off as the police and the fans faced each other. Suddenly, the crowd surged and let out a deafening roar. I could not see the cause of the surge, but I let myself flow with the crowd. In the distance, I could see a number of coaches being escorted into the car parks. The presence of a number of large orange flags on the windows indicated that the Dutch were now here. The chances were that this was just their normal supporters, but as their boys appeared to have failed to turn up, the pent up aggression of thousands of England's finest hooligans would now be released on them.

The surge didn't last for long however. The next thing I knew, I had turned and was now rushing back to where I had just come from, closely followed by a large number of riot police. The chase stopped after about a hundred yards. The riot police had formed a line across the concourse, leaving a gap of about 50 yards between them and us. Soon, bottles started flying, the sound of breaking glass encouraging the fans to advance again. Another surge at the police was met full on by the boys in blue. A large number of fans were hit by batons or bitten by police dogs. Mounted police charged into the crowd, knocking many people to the ground where they were trampled on by people running from the police. These clashes went on for about 20 minutes and although the English won a few battles, the police easily won the war.

I found myself up near one of the turnstiles where a mob of about 200 ticketless fans was trying to force their way into the ground. The police were hopelessly outnumbered and reinforcements could not be drafted in because the angry mob had blocked the pathways. One foolhardy copper climbed onto the roof of the turnstile and attempted to address the crowd. 'This is an all ticket game. All tickets are sold out. If you do not have a ticket, please disperse immediately so that fans with tickets can gain entry to the ground.'

His speech was met by a sea of spit which was literally dripping off him. At one stage I felt sorry for him as being spat on by one person is horrible enough, but to be spat on by hundreds of angry young men must have been quite humiliating for him.

The humiliation appeared to have the desired effect though. The police just seemed to give up as the boys at the front of the mob started climbing over the turnstiles, but as I got nearer to the front I could see large numbers of police on the other side of the turnstiles. I guessed that once you had climbed over you would be instantly arrested. I started to have second thoughts, but quickly realised I was in a situation from where there was no return. Just as I was about to jump over the turnstile, the large exit gates were opened from the inside by the police. The police were letting hundreds of us into the game for nothing. I was overjoyed as I charged up the stairs and onto the steep terracing.

The game finished 2-2 and was particularly memorable for the amount of stick the crowd dished out to Ruud Gullit. Gullit was one of the best players in the world at that time, but his stance on racism obviously angered sections of the English support, particularly those who harboured far right political views. There were a couple of thousand Dutch fans in the ground, all clad in bright orange gear. They were well policed by hundreds of coppers and apart from letting off a couple of flares, they caused no trouble.

After the game, the violent clashes between the English fans and the police quickly resumed as the police refused to let us wait outside the Dutch end. As mounted police rode into the crowd, we were all forced to disperse. I found myself being chased into a multi-storey car park by a number of officers. Just before entering the multi-storey, I saw a narrow stairway leading to another outside car park so I quickly changed direction and ran down these stairs, confident that I had outwitted the police who I felt sure would follow the rest of the mob into the car park. No such luck. The police had spotted my manoeuvre and two coppers followed me right across the car park. Fortunately, I managed to lose them amongst the parked coaches.

Now on my own, I decided to head home and made my way to the tube station. Luckily, I bumped into some friends on the tube and we made our way back to Waterloo, excitedly telling tales to each other about our earlier escapades. When we arrived at Waterloo we found ourselves in the midst of a pitched battle between Portsmouth and Southampton fans. Chairs and tables were being thrown across the concourse as the two bitter rivals steamed into each other. We stood to one side and watched the clashes from a safe distance. Eventually, the police managed to take control of the situation and forced the two mobs onto their respective trains back to Hampshire.

I did not go to the European Championships, but amongst the hundreds of English boys arrested or deported were a number of boys I knew from Millwall and from home. Throughout the summer, I listened in awe to the stories of running battles with hundreds of Germans, Turks and Dutch boys. My mind was made up. If these boys could be part of this scene, then so could I.

Just prior to the European Championships, England had played Scotland at Wembley in the traditional annual fixture between the auld enemies. I went to this game and as usual the Scots had taken over large parts of the West End. These drunken, kilt wearing Scots were singing and shouting all the way to Wembley. This type of behaviour had become symbolic of the Tartan Army and for years the English had let them get away with it, but 1988 was to be the first year the English really started to do something serious about rectifying this embarrassing situation.

As I walked up Wembley Way, hundreds of Scots were urinating in full view of the police who just turned a blind eye. Wembley was completely over run by drunken Scots singing anti-English songs. The few English in the area really couldn't do a lot about it, and I for one found it infuriating.

Inside the ground, things started to look up. So many Scots live in England and have always bought their tickets direct from

Wembley, so it was virtually impossible to effectively segregate the rival fans inside the old stadium. I found myself at the front of the top tier of the terracing, and far behind me, in the top corner of the terracing, was a group of a few hundred English. Just in front, and slightly to my right was another group of English. These two groups were conspicuous by their appearance. They were a lot younger than many of the Scots, a lot more sober, and a lot better dressed. The rest of this end was filled with xenophobic Scots singing songs about Bannockbum and Diego Maradona.

Just before the game started, the bulk of the English that were stood behind us made their way down the terracing to where we were stood. One of the boys was a Millwall fan and although he was casually dressed, he was also wearing a plastic Union Flag bowler hat. A few of the boys huddled around him as he took the hat off and began urinating in the hat. Once full to the brim, he walked over to one of the Scots and threw the contents of the hat straight into his face. The Scot did not flinch. He was probably so used to the stench of urine that he was not as offended as you or I might be if we found ourselves in a similar situation.

He calmly wiped his face, and looked round to see who had committed the heinous act. The Millwall boy stood in front of him as the Scot moved forward. *BANG!* A shuddering head butt landed squarely on the Millwall fan's nose, splitting it wide open. Before he had a chance to hit the deck, the rest of the English moved towards the Scot, kicking and punching in an effort to get him down on the floor. For a moment, the Scot gave as good as he got and was really holding the English at bay, and within seconds he was receiving some back up from other Scots. A full blooded terrace battle was in progress, with neither side prepared to back down. Eventually, the police moved in and separated the rival factions. The English moved quietly away, whilst the Scots continued to chant anti-England songs.

The hostile atmosphere continued throughout the game and reached boiling point when England took the lead, courtesy of a Peter Beardsley goal. The mob of English in the lower tier celebrated the goal in traditional fashion by baiting their hated rivals from north of the border. The Scots were not prepared to take any of this, and for the second time in 90 minutes a bitter battle was fought on the Wembley terraces. Despite being heavily outnumbered, the English again refused to back down.

As the end of the game approached, the Scots started to head out of the ground. I waited till the end of the match, just to make sure we had clinched the victory. I then headed out of Wembley and into the hot sunshine, still pumped full of adrenaline from the clashes I had witnessed inside. My exhilaration soon changed to deep concern though when I saw hundreds of Scots waiting menacingly on the grassy banks that surrounded the stadium. This was the first mob of quiet Scots I had seen all day and they certainly looked like they meant business. My fears escalated when I realised there were enough English around me to justify the Scots launching an attack.

I had hoped to keep my head down and prayed that the Scots would leave me out of it on the grounds that I was just a kid, but it wasn't going to be that easy. They had spotted some of the English boys they had been fighting with in the ground and charged down the banks towards us. The English scattered everywhere and I found myself being chased towards Wembley Stadium train station by hundreds of angry Scots. I ran and ran and eventually realised I was no longer being pursued.

For some reason, I started to walk back to the ground, but just before I reached the stadium, I turned left into one of the car parks. I cut through this car park and headed towards Wembley Way, but before I reached the road, I was on my toes again as another huge mob of Scots ran towards me. Were they being chased by the English? I wasn't sure, but I wasn't going to wait around to find out. Once again I ran for my life and at one stage I was very close to being dragged to the ground and beaten, but in circumstances like that, you usually manage to find that little surge of energy needed to pull yourself away from the pursuing mob.

Once the Scots had given up the chase, I took stock of the situation. There was little point heading towards Wembley Way. If I had tried, I think I would still be there now running back and forth. Instead, I went back in the direction of the station and decided to head back into London. I was still very edgy as the Scots were still everywhere, but fortunately for me, the violent mob had chosen to leave Wembley by other means. I avoided the West End and returned home, tired, exhilarated and proud that England's fans had made a stand.

My pride flourished in the morning when all the papers had photographs of the clashes inside the ground. I had been there and all my friends wanted to know the real story. The tales of the incidents outside Wembley did not go down too well though, and many of us boldly stated that we would make the return trip to Glasgow the following year to seek revenge.

Scotland, 1989

FOR ALMOST A year, there had been talk of us all going to Glasgow for the return fixture. So many of us were planning on going, there had even been talk of hiring a whole train carriage on the overnight train from London to Glasgow.

The talk came to nothing though, and I found myself strolling along the High Street at lunchtime the day before the Hampden clash with no intention of going to Scotland when I bumped into a good friend of mine called Paul. He had gone to Germany for Euro '88 and was a proud and passionate supporter of both Spurs and England.

We were chatting about the possibility of Arsenal beating Liverpool in the crunch decider for the League title, a game that was being played that very night and was to be shown live on TV. Paul was saying he would have to find a pub which was not showing the game as he could not bear to watch Arsenal play. Half jokingly, I suggested going to London and then onto Glasgow for the England game. Incredibly, we decided there and then, that we would do exactly that.

We returned home, got washed and changed, and met back at our local pub at five o' clock. I was seeing a girl at the time and she came into the pub a short while after. The previous week, I had also gone to Glasgow to watch the Rangers versus Celtic Cup Final.

'Where are we going tonight, Colin?' she asked.

'I don't know about you love, but I'm off to Glasgow with Paul.'

Her face threatened to explode with anger. This was the second week in a row I had gone off without her and I knew what was going through her mind. 'Have you met someone up there?', she asked.

I was delighted she had asked this question. 'Yeah, that's right, I have.'

Well, it was true to a certain extent. I had met a lot of people the weekend before, and I was likely to meet many more over the next couple of days. I must admit however, that I had not spoken to one girl the previous weekend and I wasn't likely to be chatting up any birds on this trip either. But if she wanted to believe different, then I was only too happy for her to go off with the hump. I took the easy way out of it and didn't give her a second thought ever again. Like most girls, she failed to realise that there are more important things on our minds when we go on international duty than trying to pull. Like protecting ourselves from our enemies for one.

The two of us set off for the short journey to London and made our way over to Victoria. Paul fancied getting a coach to Scotland and so we went over to the coach station to check out the prices. Fortunately, they were all booked up, so after a few beers in The George, we headed up to Euston to catch the midnight train to Glasgow.

By now, we had heard the news from Anfield. Arsenal had clinched the League by beating Liverpool by two clear goals, with the crucial second goal coming in the last minute. Personally, I was pleased Arsenal were bringing the championship back to London, but being a Yid, Paul was furious.

Much to my surprise, the train from London was fairly quiet, with only a handful of London fans heading to Scotland for the football. I dozed off and was awoken by the sound of laughter and banter. I looked up to see 50 or 60 casual young men making their way up our carriage. We had pulled into Coventry, and from now until Carlisle, mobs of England's finest football hooligans began boarding the train.

Although a huge mob of Blues got on at Birmingham New Street, this was nothing compared to the numbers that got on at Preston. You had the Lancashire mobs of Preston, Burnley and Wigan, the Manchester mobs, City, Stockport, Oldham and Bolton, and you also had a large number of pissed up and very boisterous Arsenal boys. A short while later, we pulled into Carlisle where the Border City Firm joined the train. Despite the presence of so many mobs, including many arch rivals, there was no hint of a bad atmosphere. A few of the Northerners were a little pissed off with the Arsenal boys, but everyone acknowledged the fact that they were celebrating a famous victory. Anyway, we were all English, and on our way to Glasgow to take on the Scots on their own manor.

As we crossed the border and the dark sky started to give way to daybreak, the carnival atmosphere changed. We were now on enemy territory. As we passed through beautiful countryside and pretty villages, derogatory remarks were made about all things Scottish. The abuse grew more and more vociferous as we approached the urban sprawl of Glasgow.

'Look at the state of them houses. I wouldn't let my dog live in a hovel like that'.

'Your dog's probably better looking than most of those soap dodging Glaswegian slags.'

The whole point of remarks such as this seemed to be to inspire hatred in Scotland and pride in England. It really worked as well. I have been to Scotland many times and found the people friendly, and the countryside glorious. However, all those pleasant thoughts had been left behind by the time the train pulled into Central Station, and I could imagine how I would feel if I was going somewhere I really do detest, like Italy or Germany.

It was only about six o'clock in the morning when a good few hundred English lads poured off the train. A few Glasgow police were present, but obviously no Scottish fans were there to greet us. What were we going to do until the pubs opened? Fortunately, a couple of English guys were waiting for us. 'If you go down the market, the pubs are open 24 hours a day,' we were told. Directions were provided and off we set, looking for a pub in Glasgow at six in the morning!

Paul needed to find a bank to get some money and I needed to find a cafe to get some breakfast. We left the main mob and headed into the deserted city centre. After a traditional Scottish fry up, we headed back in the direction the mob had been going when we had left them earlier.

As we were walking along, I noticed a group of casuals approaching us. 'Surely too early for the Jocks,' I said to Paul.

'Yeah, but be ready, just in case,' warned Paul.

'Who are youse?' shouted one of the boys from across the road.

The accent had seemed peculiar, but I knew it wasn't Scottish. There was about ten of them in total and they all looked quite up for it. Even so, it was still only 6.30 in the morning, and who wants a tear up that early?

'We're English,' I replied.

The smallest bloke in their mob crossed over into the road. 'Stoke!' he shouted, and seemed genuinely shocked when we laughed at him.

He really did look silly trying to be hard in front of his mates, and when they pulled him back and apologised to us for his behaviour, he had a face like thunder. He didn't look hard and he certainly didn't have an intimidating voice.

14

We continued walking to the market area and sure enough there were a number of pubs open. All were packed to the rafters with the English guys from our train. We managed to order a pint and started to relax. The atmosphere in the pubs was fantastic, and it soon felt like it was two o clock in the afternoon. We soon got into the routine that was to become so familiar at all England away games. You get chatting to whoever stands near you and the first thing you always ask is 'Who are you?'

The person will state the team he follows and you will state your team. If the two teams have a history of battles, these will be discussed in depth. Nine times out of ten, you always get on with the other lads. You all love football, drinking, travelling, and the buzz that goes with the trip, and therefore it stands to reason that you should all get on. On top of this, you know that at some stage there is going to be trouble and you must feel sure in yourself that the people you are with will keep an eye out for you. Some incredible friendships have been formed at England games as a result of people you barely know helping you out of life threatening situations.

Obviously, there are always the idiots who just want to start trouble with everyone they meet. You soon learn how to spot them and you try to avoid them at all costs. Then there are the funny lads. They may be idiots, but they are good company and make you laugh in the pubs and bars. However, it is best to avoid these people on the streets too because often they cannot be relied upon either if situations do get on top.

The beers were flowing and Paul and myself were chatting to a number of people, mainly boys from Preston and Birmingham. As time passed, more and more English turned up. Apart from a mob from Hemel Hempstead, there were very few Southerners in the pub so when I heard a London accent, I made a point of chatting to the two lads. 'Who are you?' I asked.

'We're Palace, who are you?' they replied in a rather aggressive way.

When I told them I was a Millwall supporter I expected a bit of grief, but to be fair to them they just started to take the piss. I had a drink with one of them whilst the other lad went off to the bar to get the drinks. They were not bad blokes, but you can only talk to Palace fans for so long before they start to irritate you.

The other lad soon returned with the beers and was chuckling to himself. 'You have got to go to the bar and talk to that div over there.'

I looked over to see a lad standing at the bar on his own. He had a gormless expression on his face and really looked out of place amongst all the boys. 'Alright mate, who are you?' I asked.

He told me that he was a Southampton fan and had organised a coach from the city. On arrival in Glasgow, most of his companions had deserted him and gone drinking elsewhere, hence the reason he was now on his own. After talking to him for a couple of minutes, it soon became obvious why his mates had left him. He was the most boring man in the world. I had already had quite a few beers and was chatting away, but he just did not appear to respond.

'You must hate Pompey, being a Scummer,' I observed. I thought the subject of Portsmouth was bound to liven up any Southampton fan, but he just seemed to be indifferent.

'They're not so bad,' he replied.

I could take no more and left him to it. Over the next hour or so, a number of different lads went over to chat to him. After a minute or so, everyone returned to their own mobs, confident that they too had met the most boring man in the world. He was quickly christened Mr Boring. The name was to stick and we were to meet up with him at other games in the future.

By 12.30, I was so drunk I could take no more ale. Although the pub was packed with English, there were also groups of Glaswegians in the pub who looked like they had been drinking all night. One of them was in his sixties and looked just like all the other Glaswegians you meet in gutters and cardboard boxes throughout London. He had run out of money and like his brethren from the cardboard boxes, he was reduced to begging off the English for enough money to buy another drink.

He approached one of the Palace fans who promised to get him a drink if he performed a rendition of 'No surrender to the IRA'. The Scot obliged and so the Palace fan had no alternative but to get him a beer. He had almost finished his own pint, so he went round the pub filling his glass with the leftover drinks from the glasses left on the tables. A concoction of lager, heavy, Guinness, whisky, vodka and gin soon filled the pint. A dash of Tabasco sauce was added to give it a kick, and being a Palace fan he also felt the need to spit into the glass for good measure. He handed the drink over to the Scot and ordered him to down it in one. Much to my disgust, the Scot easily downed the drink and even appeared to enjoy it. The thought of the drink was enough to make me sick though, and I rushed off to the toilet to throw my guts up.

16

Being sick cleared my head and I suddenly felt much better. It was two or three miles to Hampden Park from the pub, and although you could get a bus or a train to the ground, we had all decided to walk. About 60 of us set off, armed with glasses and bottles.

As we approached the city centre, my attention was drawn to a newsagents shop. One of the local papers carried a headline about English casuals arriving en masse in Glasgow. A few of us called in to buy the paper as a momento of our trip, but when we left the newsagent, we suddenly found ourselves on our own as the main bulk of our mob had continued walking. There were now four Englishmen about to walk into the centre of Glasgow, just a couple of hours before one of the most volatile clashes in the whole of football. We decided to split up in the hope that we would not be spotted if we were on our own. There was no doubt that if we stuck together, we would draw attention to ourselves and attract trouble. We also dropped our weapons.

Paul and myself kept an eye on each other as we walked about 15 yards apart. We found ourselves in a pedestrianised street full of shoppers. Everything was going okay until we heard the unmistakable sound of a Scottish football crowd. 'We fucking hate England!' they chanted as they rounded the corner and came into view. They were fully kitted out in traditional Scottish football regalia - replica shirt, tartan hats and lion rampant flags. All of them were carrying cans of lager.

As they approached us, I kept my head down and pretended to be a local out shopping on a Saturday afternoon. The smell of alcohol became almost overpowering as the Scots engulfed us. 'What a hell of a way to die, to die an English bastard!' . . . 'We hate Jimmy Hill, he's a poof . . .'

The noise was now deafening as we found ourselves in the middle of this drunken mob. My heart was pumping away. If they spotted us, there was no doubt that we would be kicked to the ground. I continued walking through the crowd, trying not to look out of place, and slowly the drunken chants started to fade as the mob passed on by.

I knew Hampden Park was on the south side of Glasgow and therefore gathered that we would need to cross the Clyde at some stage. I knew there was a bridge near Central Station and decided to head back in that direction. All the way to the Clyde, I walked with my head down, passing mobs of Glaswegians singing aggressively about all things English. My thoughts turned to the English mob we

17

had left. Where were they and how were they getting on? I had not heard the sound of fighting, but felt sure something would be happening somewhere.

My navigational skills soon paid dividends and I found myself on a bridge overlooking the Clyde. Paul and myself were chatting about our adventures in the city centre when we noticed a running battle taking place on one of the other bridges further down the river, between a mob of English and hundreds of Scots. From what I could see, the Scots charged at the English from behind, throwing bottles and other weapons. Once all their weapons had been launched, the English steamed into the Scots and chased them off the bridge back towards the city centre. The English mob then continued walking towards Hampden. We decided to join up with this mob and so ran down the street parallel to the river and joined them.

We soon got chatting to a few of these boys, most of whom were Blues, but there were a few Stockport, Preston and Plymouth boys too. There were about 80 of us in total, and we moved as one unit, keeping close together at all times. We were now on a main street, heading towards Hampden. Everywhere you looked, you were surrounded by drunken Scottish fans, chanting obscenities about the English.

We approached a pub packed with Scottish supporters. One of the Preston lads walked up to its doors and threw a gas canister inside. The people in the pub spilled out into the streets to confront us, and once again bottles and glasses were thrown at the English. Punches were exchanged before the Scots were once again chased off.

We continued our walk. Small groups of Scots would run to within 50 yards of us before launching bottles at us. Once they had thrown the bottles, they would run away before any of us could get anywhere near them. Their cowardice was both amusing and annoying. By now, all of us were so determined to hurt some Glaswegians that any Scottish fan became a target.

Our numbers by now had been swollen by a mob of about 20 lads from Rochdale who had been drinking in a pub nearby, and as we turned into another street we saw a huge mob of Scots about 200 yards in front of us. There must have been three or four hundred of them. They spotted us immediately and started moving towards us. This is it, I thought, two large mobs and no police anywhere in sight.

As the Scots moved to within bottle throwing distance, a hail of missiles was launched at us. Bottles, glasses, stones, coins and even planks of wood came flying through the air, injuring a fair few English. I protected my eyes as I waited for the barrage of missiles to come to an end. Sure enough, the missiles stopped. We picked up what we could and steamed into the Scots. For a moment they stood, but after a few punches were thrown, they were forced to retreat. Despite having the numbers, they were being chased all over their own city. We gave up the chase and continued our summer stroll to Hampden.

We soon found ourselves in a street with a number of small shops. All the shop keepers were frantically boarding up their shops, but some were too late and a few windows were smashed. The sound of police sirens grew louder and louder as the police desperately tried to reach us.

Shortly before the police arrived though, a group of seven or eight Indian shopkeepers, came out of a shop armed with knives, determined to protect their business premises. They were viciously attacked by the English, although they were quick to use their blades in their defence. The Strathclyde Police turned up in force as this knife battle took place. One English guy was dragged away by half a dozen police, kicking and fighting all the way. I felt sorry for him as I realised he would be spending the bank holiday weekend in Barlinnie Prison, an unpleasant though at the best of times.

Our mob was now under heavy police escort as we slowly walked to the ground. Once again, another huge mob of Glaswegians approached. As we were walking on the pavement, they crossed to the other side of the road and threw all of their bottles. This time they were not aiming directly at us. Their plan was to throw the bottles at the tenement buildings, thus ensuring the bottles would smash above our heads and rain glass down on us. Their plan certainly worked and I spent the next few minutes pulling pieces of glass out of my hair.

We made a counter surge towards the Scots which sent them on their toes. They need not have ran though because the police prevented us from breaking out of our escort by thumping anyone who moved. Hitting Englishmen seemed to be part of their job description and they appeared to be enjoying the day as much as we were.

We had proceeded another half a mile or so without further incident. We were kept on the pavement by scores of mounted police who were backed up by a large number of riot vans.

However, as open park land appeared on our left, our unit tried to break out of the escort and escape.

About 30 of us succeeded and gained access to the park before the police realised what was happening. I was overjoyed at having got one over on the police as Paul and myself and the rest of our little mob walked up the hill. My heart sank though when we reached the top. All I could see were hundreds of Scots singing, drinking and heading towards Hampden. A few of them spotted us immediately and roared their disapproval. This attracted the rest of the Scots and suddenly I found myself in a living nightmare.

A few of the Plymouth boys were with us and we all realised we were now in serious trouble. 'Just stand and fight. Don't fucking run from no one. Remember, we're English and better than these fuckers.' These words, spoken in a broad, Devonian accent, certainly inspired me. I felt that I would get a good kicking in the next few minutes, but I was determined to go down fighting.

The first mob of Scots approached from our left. As they bounced towards us, they were smiling, obviously looking forward to kicking some English arse. 'Come on then!', shouted one of the Plymouth boys, and as one, our unit charged towards the Scots. The expression on their faces quickly changed and despite having superior numbers, they ran for their lives. We gave up the chase and looked each other in the eyes. Our confidence was boosted by this result. Perhaps we were not going to die after all. Without hesitation, we charged down the hill towards the Scots in the centre of the park. There were hundreds of Scots there who, just a minute earlier, had been chanting about how they sent the English homeward, to think again. The roles had certainly been reversed now as 30 English chased hundreds of Scots out of the park. Without their bottles, the Glaswegians were hopeless.

Again, we gave up the chase, content in the knowledge that we had proved a point. The police had now found a way into the park and half a dozen riot vans raced towards us. They quickly rounded us up and then escorted us out of the park. Suddenly, the Scots wanted to have another go at getting to us, but the police prevented them from doing so. I felt it was just a token gesture anyway because they didn't want to know a few minutes earlier when there was nobody to prevent us from fighting.

Once out on the mean streets of Glasgow again, we could see Hampden Park in the distance, but we were held in a side street by the police for a few minutes to enable them to bring another mob of

English to join us. I recognised many of the faces in this mob from the pubs we had been drinking in earlier. Stories were exchanged as we greeted each other. The stories were basically the same. The Glaswegians just wanted to throw their bottles before running away.

At one stage though, the other mob had confronted a group of Aberdeen casuals who had actually stood and fought with the English. We were gutted at missing this rare sight. This was the first group of Scottish casuals I had heard about all day. The people we had been fighting with all day were definitely Glaswegians and definitely had no dress sense. However, it soon became apparent that Scottish casuals, primarily from Aberdeen, Edinburgh and Dundee, were in Glasgow and were quite prepared to fight for their country.

After this short break, the police continued to escort us towards Hampden. As we approached the ground, under heavy police escort, the bottle throwing started all over again, as hundreds of young, scruffy Glaswegians threw bottles from their vantage points on the grassy banks outside the ground. A few English were struck, but no efforts were made to attack the Scots. What was the point? They would only run, and by this time we were all too tired to chase after anyone.

We reached the turnstiles where a police officer with a loud hailer ordered us to have our tickets ready for inspection. No one had match tickets and this caused a bit of panic amongst the police. Eventually, they decided to allow us to gain admission by paying cash at the turnstile, a wise move in the circumstances.

Once I was inside the ground, the heat and exhaustion overtook me. I sat down on the terracing and tried to relax. The atmosphere in the ground was incredible, with the Scots making an incredible noise. However, all the singing and chanting and anti-English sentiments failed to intimidate me as much as it might have done, as the Scots had let themselves down in the streets of Glasgow. They could sing as much as they wanted to about how much they hated the English, and how it must be terrible to die an English bastard, but when it came down to it, most of them had proved themselves to be all mouth in the confrontations that had taken place outside.

As the game kicked off, I found myself drifting off to sleep. The sleepless night on the train, too much alcohol, and the running battles had all taken their toll. I was rudely awakened though by the sound of North Eastern accents and looked up to find myself in the middle of a stand off between a group of Geordies and a group of Sunderland supporters. I quickly woke Paul up who had nodded off too, and we both scurried to safety as the fierce rivals confronted each other. We then found ourselves in the middle of a group of Boro supporters. They had spotted a mob of Hibs fans in the Scottish section next to us who they had been fighting earlier on in the day and were keen to resume the battle. They surged towards the fence that separated the rival fans and made a gallant effort to climb over it. The police were having none of it though, and pushed the Boro fans back off the fence. They were not too downhearted though. Hibs could wait for later.

England won the game 2-0, with goals from Chris Waddle and Steve Bull. As it turned out, it was to be the last of the annual fixtures between the two sides. It was decided that following the events in Glasgow in 1987 and 1989, and the usual destruction that takes place in London, the security risks were becoming too severe to justify playing these games. However, this was not the end of the story for we still had to get back to the centre of Glasgow after the game.

We were kept in the ground for 45 minutes after the final whistle while the police dispersed the home supporters from the immediate vicinity of the ground. We were let out of the ground under heavy police escort and began the slow, long walk back to Glasgow.

The police had done a good job, and there were very few Scots in sight. However, after about 15 minutes, a group of Scots were spotted down a side street. 'We are the English football hooligans!' roared the crowd as a number of English attempted to charge down the road. They were prevented from doing so though by the heavy handed tactics of the Strathclyde Police. Their fondness of battering Englishmen was starting to annoy many of us, and the atmosphere between the police and their prisoners became very volatile.

As we approached the Clyde, we were stopped and addressed by a mounted police officer with a loud hailer. 'When you get back to Glasgow, you will all be put on trains back to England. Anyone who tries to go into the city centre will be arrested, sent to Barlinnie, and will appear in court on Tuesday. Those of you from Lancashire, the Midlands and London stay here. You will be taken to Central Station where a train is waiting to take you home. Those of you from the North East, Yorkshire or the East Midlands, come with me. You will be taken to Queen Street where a train is also waiting to take you home.'

I waited while the Geordies and Yorkies made their way to Queen Street. After a short delay, we continued to Central Station, our numbers now reduced by half. The area around the station was quite deserted, but as our train was not ready for us, we were forced to wait in a side street near the station. No Glaswegians made any attempt at ambushing us, although it was obviously still kicking off elsewhere as you could hear the sound of fighting and police sirens going towards Queen Street. Although it made sense to split the English into two groups, it was obvious that large groups of Scottish casuals from Edinburgh and Aberdeen would be waiting at Queen Street. I later heard that serious disorder took place in and around Queen Street and also later in Edinburgh. On these occasions, the English faced tougher opposition as the Edinburgh and Aberdeen gangs actually prefer fighting to throwing bottles.

Eventually, our train arrived and we were herded into Central Station and forced to board the train. Paul and I found ourselves in a carriage packed full of Blues. They had taken a large mob to Scotland and were certainly one of the most active firms there that day. They were well pleased with their turn out, and luckily for me, they were all in a good frame of mind.

The train was so slow that I knew by the time it reached London it would be late and I would have difficulty getting home so some of the Blues we'd been talking to offered to put us up in Birmingham for the night. We accepted what seemed to be a kind and genuine offer, but I still went to the toilet and stuffed my money down my pants, just in case of trouble later on.

We arrived in Birmingham just before closing time and headed towards a pub in the city centre. We then jumped in cabs to take us to where these boys lived in Birmingham. Although they seemed genuine enough, I was still nervous when the cab dropped us off in the middle of a large housing estate somewhere in Birmingham, long after midnight. As it turned out, I had a good night's kip before going to their local for a Sunday lunch time booze. When the pub shut at three o'clock, they ordered us a taxi to New Street and saw us off on the train back to London.

It had been a wonderful ending to a weekend that will stay with me forever. These boys had shown genuine friendship to people they barely knew. I soon became aware that this type of behaviour was typical amongst many of the English fans who regularly travel abroad to watch England play. I enjoyed the trip to Scotland so much that I began saving up for the trip to Italy to watch England play in the World Cup in 1990.

England still had to qualify though, and we faced two crucial games in Sweden and Poland before qualification could be guaranteed. The game in Sweden will always be remembered by many for the brave performance of Terry Butcher who played on despite suffering a serious head injury. His white England shirt was covered in blood, but still he refused to give in to the Swedes. The English fans were also not giving in to anyone, and a series of skirmishes took place in Stockholm before, during, and after the game. At one stage, the head of Stockholm police warned local citizens to stay in until the English had left the country. I watched the scenes on TV and laughed as I recognised faces I knew from Coventry, Cheltenham and Carlisle. I regretted the fact that I had not gone, but comforted myself with the idea of a fortnight in Sardinia the following summer.

To guarantee qualification, England needed to secure a point in Katowice against the Poles. A few lads I knew made the trip to Poland. The beer and vodka was cheap, England drew 0-0, and the locals were more than game for a row. In addition, they got to do a bit of sightseeing at Auschwitz of all places.

The draw for the group stages was made in December, 1989, and England were to play on the island of Sardinia against Ireland, Holland and Egypt. I couldn't wait.

Italia 1990

FOLLOWING THE DRAW for the World Cup, numerous people told me that they wanted to come to Sardinia with me. The media were full of reports about how the Italian authorities would refuse you admission to Sardinia if you did not have tickets for the games. None of us had tickets and none of us were intending to try to obtain tickets through the official channels either.

I scanned the holiday brochures looking for suitable accommodation. England were to play their games in Cagliari, the capital of Sardinia. This city was a bustling port and really didn't seem the place to spend your summer holiday. The east coast of Sardinia was where many of the resorts were located and they were all pretty exclusive, with prices to match. My attention was then drawn to the resort of Alghero in the north west of the island. The prices were affordable and the resort looked quite nice.

Ten of us booked up for the trip, although we could not travel on our chosen dates. The only available dates meant that we arrived in Alghero one week before our opening match against Ireland. It also meant we would miss the final group game against Egypt.

We paid the deposit on the holiday, but by the time we were due to pay the balance six of the lads had dropped out. This left two Arsenal fans, Dean and Tom, and a West Ham fan by the name of Ady as my travelling companions.

We arrived at Gatwick airport late on the Monday night, in plenty of time for the early morning flight to Sardinia. We settled down in one of the 24 hour pubs in the terminal to waste away the hours, slowly getting drunk. Eventually, we boarded our plane and were pleased to see a dozen or so other England fans also on the flight.

As the plane circled over the small international airport at Alghero, our thoughts turned to the holiday rep who was due to meet us on the other side of customs. Ady was adamant that he would be getting inside her knickers at some stage over the fortnight, and he wasn't the only one with ideas in that direction. We passed through customs without any problems, despite the threats that had been made about refusing admission to ticketless fans. However, our joy at being allowed into the country was soon replaced by a feeling of horror when we saw the state of the rep who was waiting for us.

She was the spitting image of Barbara Woodhouse and talked to us in the same manor as Barbara spoke to one of her naughty puppies. She ordered us on to the coach that was to take us to the resort, and she soon started to give us a list of instructions. There was no warm welcome or useful advice about things to do, places to see or the usual holiday rep waffle. Instead, we were ordered to be polite to the Sardinians at all times, not to drink to excess, not to sunbathe, not to hire a car, and most important of all, we were told that under no circumstances should we attempt to travel to Cagliari without a ticket for the game. We were warned that the local prison was only a few miles out of town and that we would all be sent there if we misbehaved. By all accounts, the conditions in this jail were horrendous. This woman was doing a better job of scaring the travelling English support than Colin Moynihan and his cronies at Number Ten.

We settled into our apartments and within the hour a number of Union flags were hanging off the balconies. Chingford, Arsenal, West Ham, Notts County and Bradford were all represented. The day was spent lazing around the pool getting to know the other English lads. There was a group of boys from Bradford, Grimsby, Huddersfield and various other places throughout England. Arrangements were made to head into town together that night since none of us knew exactly what to expect.

The old town itself was very pretty with many chic boutiques and bars battling for space in the narrow streets. About a dozen of us stuck together all night and everywhere we went we were stared at by locals, both male and female. Every barman was unfriendly and every waiter was slow and rude. The Italians treated us with contempt and we made no effort to change their preconceived ideas and opinions. The police also followed us from bar to bar. Occasionally, Italians would drive by on their mopeds and yell abuse at us whilst making the cut-throat gesture with their hands.

The following night we were sat outside a bar in the town square, enjoying a quiet drink. Word had obviously got around the town that some of the England fans had now arrived. About a hundred yards away, on the other side of the square, a large group of locals started to gather. It wasn't a mob in the normal sense - I think they had just come to look at the English. There were even quite a few girls with them.

We started to feel like animals in a zoo, being stared at and talked about like this. We decided to make a point. We quietly spoke to each other and agreed that at a given signal, we would stand as one, pick up our chairs, and pretend to attack them. A few minutes later, the signal was given and we all stood up and roared. Without hesitation, the large group of Italians scattered across the square in blind panic. We hadn't even moved! We fell about laughing, and when the Italians slowly drifted back into the square, they were not quite as cocky and were certainly a lot more apprehensive. The police had witnessed these events and were obviously not happy at our show of bravado.

The first few days were spent lazing around on the glorious white sandy beach and drinking plenty of lager at night. We also watched the opening games of the tournament and were overjoyed when Argentina lost to Cameroon. Italy's first game was against Austria and we all decided to watch this game together in one of the bars in the old town.

We arrived in plenty of time for kick-off, but the bar was already packed with locals. As the game kicked off, we cheered every Austrian pass and booed every intelligent or skilful contribution by the Italians. We generally just tried to annoy the Italians as much as we possibly could. It worked quite well too, until Schillaci scored in the 79th minute. We left and found another bar, but within a matter of minutes, the air was filled with the sounds of tooting horns as hundreds of Sardinians took to the street to celebrate the Italian victory.

We left the bar to see what was happening and it really was quite a sight. Young Italians were hanging out of car windows waving scarves and flags, and chanting 'Forza Italia!' Two or three people were on each moped that drove by too. They were trying to taunt us, but made sure they kept a safe distance from us at all times. A few bottles were thrown at the Italians, but that was about it because the police forced us to return to the bar.

At the end of every night, we would walk along the sea front back to our accommodation. Italians on mopeds would drive by, threatening to kill us, and sometimes throwing stones. At all times they made sure they were out of harm's way. This cowardly behaviour happened every night and was really starting to wind us up. If they really wanted to fight, then there were plenty of opportunities, but it seemed to me that all Italians were cowards.

27

Our opening game of the tournament was against the Republic Of Ireland. Most of the Irish fans had based themselves on the island of Sicily so we had not met any Irish fans prior to the day of the game. We managed to hire a minibus for the day and set off for Cagliari early in the morning. The drive took us through the centre of the island and took about two hours. We had been warned that police would be positioned along all main routes into the city, checking whether the English had tickets, but once again this proved to be crap.

We parked the minibus on the main street, opposite the docks, about half a mile from the station, an area that was packed with English and Irish fans. Every where you looked, there were nervous looking policemen, anxiously holding their pistols and tear gas rifles. The Irish and the English were all together but despite the general friendliness of the Irish fans, the English were not really interested in socialising.

Different groups of English fans were talking to each other and most made no attempt to befriend the Irish. Most of the English fans had been staying in the campsites around Cagliari and their stories revolved around dirty campsites in the middle of nowhere, with nowhere to go and nothing to do. On top of this, the police were on their case all day and all night. If the fans did manage to venture into Cagliari, the Italians would verbally abuse them in much the same way as their friends in Alghero. The only time an English fan was in any danger of getting hurt would have been if he'd been caught on his own. In comparison, where we were staying sounded much better - plenty of bars, plenty of untouchable women, and lovely beaches.

As kick-off approached, the atmosphere started to liven up. 'You'll never beat the Irish!' was met by 'No surrender to the IRA!'. The Irish were in party mood, but the English were slowly becoming more and more aggressive.

We left the bars around the station and set off for the ground which was apparently a couple of miles away. A large group of us, about 300, slowly started to walk to the ground. We walked along the docks and after about a mile or so, a large church appeared on our left, high up on a hill, with steps leading up to it. A large group of Irish were sat on the steps, taking in the evening sunshine. As we approached, the Irish started to taunt us. 'You'll never beat the Irish!', they chanted.

No doubt they thought they were just getting involved in some friendly banter between rival fans, but they obviously had no comprehension of the mentality of most English fans, and in particular, the fans that travel abroad with England. To us, they were taking the piss, a situation that could not be tolerated. 'No surrender to the IRA!' we roared in defiance, before charging up the steps towards the Irish. They really did not expect this kind of reaction from us and fled in panic. The police, who had surrounded us on the street below, now began to chase us up the steps towards the church. As I reached the top, I noticed that a wedding was taking place. The wedding party was outside the church posing for photographs as hundreds of English fans ran through them, throwing bottles back at the police who were in hot pursuit.

Eventually, the police gave up chasing us and we continued the long walk to the ground. We soon mobbed up again and as we approached the stadium, the police converged on us. As they approached, we made a run for it across empty wasteland. Where we were running to and even why we were running at all, I wasn't quite sure, but we eventually made it to the match in one piece.

We had all purchased tickets from a tout near the train station for reasonable prices and made our way into the stadium. The stadium was disappointing - a large, soulless concrete bowl. There were certainly more Irish in the ground than English and they were easily out-singing us too. This only lasted until the ninth minute though, when Gary Lineker bundled the ball into the back of the net. The celebrations were intense as we taunted the Irish. Even when a freak thunderstorm erupted, our spirits could not be broken. Until, that is, Kevin Sheedy equalised in the 73rd minute.

In all honesty, It had been a rather dull game and the Irish certainly seemed happier with the draw than the English. At least, it meant they could continue relentlessly chanting 'You'll never beat the Irish!' at the English fans.

We had met some familiar faces from Arsenal, Chelsea and Millwall during the game, and they had decided to come back to Alghero with us that night. We all walked back to the station and although we were followed for a short while by a small group of Italian skinheads, nothing too exciting happened.

We then made our way to the station where the other lads recovered their bags from left luggage. I had the keys for the minibus and so three of us walked along the docks to dump the bags in the minibus. There were plenty of local skinheads mobbing up along this road, apparently preparing to attack the English congregating outside the station. I felt a little anxious as I walked past these skinheads, but luckily there were plenty of police around and nothing happened.

We made it back to the station in one piece and soon found ourselves in the middle of a mob of English fans, surrounded by riot police. Everyone knew that there were Italian skinheads in the area and we all wanted the opportunity of getting hold of them. After a while, the skinheads approached. We tried to breakthrough the police line, but as soon as we moved the skinheads turned and ran. The Italian police were more game though and baton charged us back into the station.

After this short but violent confrontation, a lot of the English started jumping on trains and buses back to their campsites. We decided to head off back to our minibus which unfortunately was parked up in the direction the skinheads had fled. We watched our backs all the way to the minibus, but the skinheads were nowhere to be seen. Once safely in the minibus, we began the long drive back to Alghero in the dark. We found our way onto the motorway okay, but at some stage we must have missed the Alghero turn off. The morning sun was slowly starting to rise when we noticed a local farmer walking down the deserted street with two buckets of water. The minibus pulled over and eight Englishmen jumped out and confronted the bewildered man. 'Scuse us mate, how do you get to Alghero?'

Surprisingly, the Sardinian farmer did not understand the South London accent and, much to our annoyance, was not very helpful. 'Bloody thick Italian bumpkin!' was the general consensus of opinion amongst our group. Eventually, we managed to find our resort and arrived back just in time for breakfast, and then spent the rest of the day sleeping on the beach.

Over the next few days, more and more England fans started to arrive in Alghero. A large bunch of Manchester United and Stockport County lads from Stockport was now staying in our apartments and a large mob of Aston Villa had also arrived, along with groups from Boro and Oldham. There were also a couple of Chelsea fans who kept us amused with their ridiculous lies and exaggerations.

The day time activities centred around the beach and the beach bar. Huge games of football would take place, with no rules and plenty of whole hearted tackles. Other lads would sit by the beach bar, drinking lager and talking about football and violence. All the different supporters got on with each other and at no stage was there any animosity.

A day or two later, a few of us were walking along the sea front towards the beach bar. Suddenly, a moped carrying two Italians, one driving the other carrying a large plank of wood, raced round the corner and on past us. As we rounded the same corner, a mob of England fans was running down the road trying to catch up with the moped. Apparently, the moped had pulled up by the beach and the passenger had run over to an English fan lying on the beach and attacked him with the piece of wood. He quickly returned to the moped and the two cowards managed to ride off, with the mob of angry Englishmen in hot pursuit. If we had witnessed these events we would have been in a position to force the moped to crash and if those two Italians had been caught, they would have been lucky to escape with their lives.

Later on, a few of us were sunbathing on the beach, watching the football, drinking lager, and admiring the pulling techniques of the American sailors whose ship was in port. An African approached us carrying a sports holdall which was full of fake Lacoste polo shirts. He wanted us to buy the shirts so a couple of us examined the quality of the material, pretending to be genuinely interested, while another guy emptied the contents of the holdall from behind the African's back and efficiently distributed the shirts to the rest of the English on the beach.

After a detailed examination, we told the African that we were not interested in purchasing the shirts and handed them back to him. He went to place them back in his holdall and discovered that it was empty. He looked around the beach, but the English continued playing football, oblivious to his concerns. He looked at us, but our baby like faces were pictures of innocence. He left the beach fuming, and once he had gone we all tried on our new fake designer shirts.

Every day, groups of American sailors would arrive on the beach. These men were incredibly fit, tanned and immensely attractive to the Italian girls sunbathing there. Many English guys had made pathetic attempts at seducing these gorgeous Italian girls, but the combination of red sunburnt skin, beer bellies, smelly breath, and broad northern accents failed to tempt the girls out of their bikinis. Much to our dismay, the yanks were having considerably more luck.

With the presence of ever larger numbers of English fans, the nights were becoming livelier. We had found one bar that was quite popular with many of us. The bar staff were keen football fans and were all quite chatty. On top of this, there was also a small dance floor. Their taste of music was rather disappointing though. It was basically limited to Elvis, Rod Stewart and Abba. To be fair to the landlord, he offered to play any tapes that we had and so the following night we all turned up, armed with one Madness tape.

The DJ had obviously never heard of Suggs and Co., but was only too willing to play the tape. The first song to be played was *Bed And Breakfast Man* and instantly the dance floor was packed as we all danced and generally made fools of ourselves. The local police steamed straight into the bar, waving their batons provocatively in our faces. The music was turned off and a fierce row developed between the police and the barman. The barman eventually came over to us and apologised, saying that the police had instructed him to shut the bar for the night.

We moved onto another bar and continued drinking. There were a lot of American sailors in this bar, drinking and chatting to the Italian girls. We started talking loudly about the Vietnam War in a bid to wind up the Yanks. Before long, the words to *Born In The USA* were changed to *Fucked In Vietnam* as a large number of us took to singing. Fortunately, the Yanks ignored us and continued pulling the local girls.

A few nights later, Italy played USA in their second group match. As there were now hundreds of England fans in the resort, the chances of trouble erupting when the Italians took to the street after the game was high. As it turned out, the Italians struggled against USA, only winning by one goal to nil. Immediately after the final whistle, the tooting horns started as hundreds of mopeds and cars took to the streets. We continued drinking in the bar, when a small group of Italians came in. 'Forza Italia!' they chanted. The barman came over, obviously concerned at the situation. 'That is Mad Dog', he warned.

The barman had already told us about Mad Dog. He was a local face and had a bit of a reputation in the town. One of the big Boro lads, Nigel, went straight over to Mad Dog, put his right hand to his throat and lifted him of his feet. He held him by his throat for a few seconds until the colour drained from his face. Then he threw him out of the bar, down the stairs and onto the street below. Mad Dog's friends quickly left the bar and picked their leader up from the ground, a wise move because Nigel was in no mood to put up with any nonsense from mouthy Italians.

We all left the bar and headed out into the town square. The Italians continued to bait us and even though we were followed by the police, we made a few half hearted attempts at charging the Italians. Before we had covered five yards though, the Italians had scattered leaving us prone to attack from the police. Not surprisingly, we soon became disillusioned with the fun and games. About 15 of us decided to firm up and go looking for Italians elsewhere. We felt that a mob of Italians might be prepared to mix it if they outnumbered us. We walked round for 20 minutes or so, but failed to come across any mob who were up for it.

We walked home that night mob handed, just in case any Italians were on the look out for stragglers. There was about 30 or so of us. The Southerners consisted of Arsenal, Millwall and Chelsea fans, and the Northerners were Villa, Oldham and Boro. About 50 yards in front of us was the group of lads from Stockport, who were also staying in our apartments. We were all very drunk. A few of the Villa lads jumped on the wall and started yelling abuse at the Stockport lads. They were a good set of lads and turned round to give us some stick back. A few of them chanted for Stockport whilst the rest chanted for Manchester United.

United are not the most popular team amongst most English fans and this seemed to wind up a few boys in our group. The Villa lads responded by chanting about the Munich air disaster, a subject all United fans find offensive despite the fact that they sing similar songs to Liverpool fans concerning the death of Bill Shankly. The United lads turned round and started to come towards us. They were well game and it looked like a huge tear up was about to kick off. This would have been a great shame as we were all getting on so well.

Fortunately, one of the Villa fans lost his footing and fell off the wall, landing on his face and clearly injuring himself quite seriously. We all burst out laughing, and fortunately this appeared to quell the situation. The United fans accepted that justice had been seen to be done and we all went home together. The following morning we all apologised to the United lads and the subject was not mentioned again.

The night before the Holland game, we were sat drinking in a quiet bar in the old town. There were a couple of blokes sat at the end of the bar and one of them had a face that rang a few bells with me. It was Mr Boring who I had met in Glasgow the previous year. I was chatting to Joe, an Arsenal fan from Walthamstow, when I realised who it was. 'You've got to meet that lemon over there, he's the most boring bloke in the world'.

Joe and myself strolled over to Mr Boring. 'Alright mate?' I enquired. 'You were in Dirty Den's East Enders bar in Glasgow last year, you're Southampton aren't you?'

'Yeah, that's right, how're you doing?' he replied.

At least he was friendly. His mate just stared at us, trying hard to look menacing. We ignored him and Joe got stuck into the conversation. 'Did you go to Spurs away, last game of the season?' he asked.

'Yeah, I was there', he replied.

'Any good?' asked Joe, obviously enquiring as to whether there had been any bother at the game.

'No,' he replied, 'we hit the post in the last minute and . . . '

While Mr Boring recalled the move that led to the shot that hit the woodwork, Joe and myself were choking on our drinks. Mr Boring didn't realise we were laughing at him, but Mr Menacing did. He was not a happy man, to say the least. Liam, a Millwall fan who was staying with us, was sat at the bar and had seen what was happening. He came over and spoke to Mr Menacing. 'You're a Southampton fan aren't you?' he said.

'Yeah, why, have you got a problem with that?' replied Mr Menacing who was now starting to look a little anxious.

'Tell me, do you drive an Escort convertible?' asked Liam.

'Yeah, I do,' Mr Menacing replied, now starting to worry as to where this line of questioning was leading.

'First day of the season, we were being escorted to Southampton station after the game. You drove by in the car and started giving it the big one. It was me and my firm that smashed your car up.'

Mr Menacing went bright red. He obviously wanted to steam in to Liam, but knew that his chances of getting out of the bar alive were minimal. Liam, Joe and myself went back to the bar to enjoy the rest of the night, while the gruesome twosome sulked in the corner.

We woke early the following morning. I prepared some ham rolls while two of the other lads went off to pick up the hire cars. All the minibuses were already booked up and we ended up with one car and one open top jeep. Four of us went in the car and the others jumped in the jeep.

Shortly after we set off on the long drive, I dished out the ham rolls that I had lovingly prepared earlier. Barry, the Arsenal boy who was driving, started moaning about the quality of the rolls, oblivious to the fact that I had prepared them. 'Those fucking wops didn't even put any butter in these rolls.'

I kept quiet in the back seat, admiring the views.

As we approached Cagliari, the driver and front passenger screamed in absolute terror. I looked around, searching for Mafia snipers at the side of the road. The cause of such fear soon became apparent. A wasp had flown through the side window and was flying around the inside of the car while everyone frantically protected themselves from being stung. The wasp managed to fly out of the open window, and we relaxed as we contemplated taking on the notorious Dutch hooligans. The thought of getting stung by a wasp was certainly more scarier than the Dutch, that much was for sure.

We met up with our friends in the jeep and couldn't help but noticed that all of them were looking like Red Indian chiefs. They had failed to realise they were getting sunburnt whilst driving along because the breeze had been keeping them cool. They shot off looking for a shop that sold Aftersun lotion and ice cold bottles of water.

We made our way to the station, where thousands of England fans were killing time. All the bars were shut and most of the English were stood chatting to each other, just trying to pass the time of day until kick-off. I walked along the docks, searching for a ticket tout. There were plenty of touts plying their trade and the police were not bothering them. I secured a ticket easily enough and headed back to the station.

On my way back I became aware of hundreds of journalists and news teams desperately seeking interviews with England fans. They were waiting for the inevitable outbreak of trouble, but their presence was annoying the bulk of the English. I noticed an American TV crew interviewing the Aston Villa lad who had fallen off the wall a couple of nights earlier when he was drunkenly abusing the Manchester United fans. His face was covered in cuts and grazes from the fall and he had obviously grabbed the attention of the pretty American woman presenting the show.

She asked him how he had sustained the injuries to his face. He told her that he had been sitting in a restaurant with his wife and kids a few nights ago, enjoying a pizza meal with his family. The next thing he knew, the police had burst in and ordered all the English people to lie face down on the ground. He objected to this breach of his civil liberties and refused to lie down. He was then viciously assaulted by the police in front of his screaming wife and children. The Americans were visibly moved by the horror of this story. I had to walk away before my laughter gave the game away.

I returned to the station where the bulk of the English were waiting. A number of people were slagging off a mob of West Ham fans who were stood on their own, avoiding contact with the rest of the English support. Apparently, they had been involved in some bother with some Bolton fans, but their general arrogance was annoying the rest of the English. We left them to their own devices.

A number of lads were walking around and telling us that we were all to march to the stadium together. They appeared to want to take the credit for organising the England mob. Although their behaviour annoyed me, their wish came true. Suddenly, all the English started walking along by the docks in the general direction of the stadium. We were closely followed by herds of journalists and even more police. Most of the English were enjoying their moment of fame and began singing the national anthem.

Just prior to reaching the church where the trouble had started before the Ireland game the previous week, the police made an effort to halt the progress of the mob. The reason for this was unclear, but rumours started flying around that a mob of Dutch boys was waiting for us further ahead. The mood of the crowd quickly turned violent. The boys at the front of the mob threw bottles while a surge from the back of the crowd forced those in front to press up against the police line.

The police panicked and baton charged the English fans onto wasteland by the side of the road. The English regrouped and started arming themselves with rocks, stones and bottles. These missiles were thrown at the police who reacted by firing tear gas canisters into the crowd. This helped to disperse the majority of the crowd, but some English lads just picked up the cartridges and flung them back in the direction of the police.

The police launched another baton charge, but this time the English stood their ground. When the English failed to run, the police panicked again. Seeing the fear in their eyes, the English seized the moment and charged at the police, who turned and ran. The feeling of euphoria was intense, but we all knew it would not last. The police regrouped and launched more tear gas canisters into the crowd. They also started firing their guns in the air.

This time, the majority of English were chased across the wasteland. A number of fans were caught and were ruthlessly assaulted by the police. A few English fans bravely went to the aid of one fan who was taking a particularly savage beating. The police were attacked and when one of them hit the floor, his pistol was taken from him and he was shot. Luckily for him, the pistol only contained blanks.

The police had now forced most of us into the back streets, behind the church. This appeared to be quite a respectable neighbourhood and many of the local residents were now leaning over their balconies, keeping an eye on the strange events unfolding below them. A series of running battles continued with the English regrouping after every charge, tooling up with bottles, and throwing them at the police.

After a few minutes of running back and forth, we found ourselves at a T junction on top of a hill. The police launched another wave of tear gas canisters and then charged towards us. This time they seemed to have organised themselves a lot better. There were hundreds of them steaming towards us. It was our turn to panic and many of the fans scattered down the two streets to our left and right. The bulk of the fans, myself included, ran straight over the junction and down the hill.

The police gave up the chase at the top of the hill as we regrouped opposite a garage. Suddenly, we turned round to see hundreds of riot police marching up the hill towards us. The police had outwitted us and now had us surrounded. Instead of charging towards us, both sets of police slowly marched towards us. We were well and truly trapped.

A few fans tried to jump over the fences next to the garage and into the gardens of the local houses. The police spotted them and charged towards us, baton charging us into the forecourt of the garage. We were all crushed into the small forecourt and had nowhere to run to, as the police battered everyone they could possibly reach. Screams of pain filled the air as heads were smashed open by the force of the assault. One fan suffered a terrible fracture to the leg as he lay crushed on the floor. After a while, the beatings stopped and we were ordered to sit down with our hands on our heads. Those who failed to sit down instantly were physically forced to sit down by the use of batons on their upper bodies.

These running battles had gone on for some time and many of the fans were breathless, injured, and choking as a result of inhaling tear gas. A few of the local residents tried to offer us bottles of water, but their kind efforts were thwarted by the police. The press, who had been present throughout the skirmishes, were now ordered to leave the area. This development concerned me. What were the police going to do to us that was so bad the press had to be removed from the area? I felt there were too many of us to be arrested so deportation was the most likely outcome.

We were kept on the garage forecourt for some time. Eventually, we were made to get up and were split into two groups. We were then taken to the stadium under heavy police escort.

Once at the ground, I purchased some bottles of water at an extortionate price and settled down to watch the game. I was just relieved to be in the ground and not on a plane home or in a Sardinian prison. England played very well and were unfortunate not to secure a victory. Goals by Lineker and Pierce were disallowed and a young and fit Paul Gascoigne easily outclassed Gullit and friends. The atmosphere was fantastic, with the Dutch fans dressed all in orange, banging drums and singing throughout the game. Once again, the Dutch supporters appeared to consist entirely of families. There was certainly no sign of their notorious hooligans.

We left the ground and headed back to the train station. I fully expected more trouble, but this time the police appeared to be in control of the situation. Although thousands of Dutch fans were at the game, most of them had flown into Cagliari on the day of the match or had sailed over from Sicily, just prior to kick-off. The police escorted them back to the port or the airport while we made our own way back to the train station. Plenty of English were hanging around waiting for something to happen, but I had seen enough for one day and decided to return to Alghero.

We had a few days of our holiday left and these were spent drinking and lazing on the beach. On the final night, we decided to go on a bender and as the alcohol took over our bodies, we realised that none of us had managed to hit one Italian, despite constant provocation. We decided to do something about this and after the bars had closed, we walked around in search of a group of Italians. We walked for ages and found ourselves in the middle of an estate.

A cyclist rode by and pulled over just up the road. 'Come on then, where's your boys?' we demanded.

He had no idea what we were talking about and scurried off into his flat, leaving his push bike at our mercy. In our anger, it was thrown across the street. We headed off home to sober up. In the morning, when we were discussing our antics the previous night, we were all embarrassed by our behaviour.

One of our group stayed on for the Egypt game, but the rest of us flew home to watch the rest of the tournament on TV back in England. As we sat on the plane at Alghero airport, we started to become impatient at the delay in taking off. The pilot apologised for the delay and explained it was due to the fact that he had to wait for the arrival of some unwanted passengers. He explained that a few English fans had let themselves and their country down. They had been arrested and were now being deported on our flight.

Shortly after his explanation, a police van screeched to a halt on the tarmac and a number of England fans boarded our plane. We recognised these lads as Bradford supporters we had met at the start of the trip. We hadn't seen them for a few days and had assumed they had moved on to another resort. We greeted them like long lost brothers, much to the disgust of the cabin crew.

My first experience of watching England on the Continent had been most enjoyable. I could not wait for the chance to travel abroad again. And fortunately, I didn't have long to wait.

I returned home to England brimming with tales of our exploits in Sardinia. The tournament was still in the group stages and it felt strange talking about something in the past tense when it was still happening. I watched England struggle to beat Egypt 1-0, courtesy of a Mark Wright goal, in my local pub. This unimpressive victory still meant that England finished top of the group ahead of Ireland and Holland.

For the first time in this tournament, England would be playing on the Italian mainland and thousands of England fans prepared to leave Sardinia for the delights of mainland Italy. Our next game was against a productive and efficient Belgian side, to be played in the Renato Dall' stadium in Bologna. The English made their way to this part of the country, but rather than head straight to Bologna, many chose to spend a few days in the brash seaside resort of Rimini, a short distance from Bologna.

The night before the England game, Italy played Uruguay in their own second round match. Goals by Schillachi and Serena secured a comfortable victory and ensured Italy would proceed to the quarter finals.   Thousands of Italians took to the streets throughout the country, waving flags and tooting horns. Meanwhile in Rimini, hundreds of England fans were watching the match on TV screens in the English style pubs in the centre of Rimini. As the Italians approached the pubs, full scale disorder broke out between the England fans, Italy fans and the police. Once again, tear gas canisters were fired at the England fans who were clearly taking the blame for the violence. The Italians had confronted the English, the English had reacted, and still the police attacked the England fans. An all too familiar story.

Despite TV evidence showing single Englishmen being viciously assaulted by dozens of riot police, the English media reacted in their normal hysterical manner. Colin Moynihan called for the English fans to be arrested and imprisoned in Italy. Curiously enough, a number of England fans were rounded up by the police and taken to the airport, where the Italian authorities just so happened to have a plane ready and waiting to fly to England. It was also uncanny how the number of people who had to be deported matched the number of seats available on a jumbo jet.

The press and our sports minister failed to understand the significance of these events.   The Italian authorities obviously wanted rid of some England fans and took this opportunity to deport over 200 of them. A diabolical liberty at the best of times, but the English government failed to take any action. After all, Englishmen who travel abroad to watch football are scum in the eyes of English politicians.

One sad but still funny tale that came out shortly after this incident was the story of an Englishman on holiday in Rimini with his wife. He had no interest in football whatsoever and had spent the evening in his hotel room with his wife. He decided to nip down to the local shop to buy some cigarettes and was grabbed by the police, bundled into a van, taken to the airport and flown home to England. When he failed to return from his shopping trip, his wife naturally became concerned. Had he been mugged or assaulted? Had he had an accident or was he lying in a gutter, bleeding to death? All these horrible thoughts must have crossed her mind that night. In the morning, she saw her husband on the news walking through an airport terminal building in England, surrounded by dozens of police while the reporter branded him an English football hooligan.

I recognised a few of the faces on the news, and the fact that the bulk of England fans were still in Italy brought it home to me that I was still missing the excitement of being over there. The following night, England struggled against a solid Belgian team, but in the final minute of extra time, David Platt scored a wonderful winner. This goal secured Platt's future for life and also meant that England had reached the quarter finals of the tournament.

Our next opposition was to be Cameroon, the surprise package of the tournament so far. The game was to be played in the San Paolo stadium in Naples, reputedly the most violent city in Italy. The English fans left Bologna and Rimini and headed south, and while they made this long journey, I made the short journey to my local travel agent. I was quietly confident we would beat the Africans, and if so, that meant we would face a semi-final in Turin, against Czechoslovakia or Germany. The Cameroon game was to be played on the Sunday night, and if all went to plan, our semi-final would be in Turin on the following Wednesday. I purchased two flight tickets from Heathrow to Turin on the Monday evening at a cost of £160 each. My friend, Paul, was to be my travelling companion. The tickets were non-refundable - if England failed to beat Cameroon, I would be out of pocket.

I watched the game in my local pub and was overjoyed when England took the lead in the 25th minute courtesy of a David Platt header. My joy turned to horror when Cameroon equalised and then took the lead. My excitement at returning to Italy and the thought of losing £160 sent me into deep depression. This depression was not lifted until the 83rd minute when England were awarded a penalty. Lineker grabbed this lifeline and coolly placed the ball in the back of the net. The game went into extra time, and in the 104th minute another penalty was awarded. Once again Lineker struck the ball into the back of the net. The celebrations in Naples were mirrored in pubs and clubs throughout England. 'Let's all have a disco!' sung the fans and players alike.

Football fever grabbed the country. A huge match against old rivals Germany was the only thing preventing us from reaching a World Cup final for the first time since 1966.

I went into work on the Monday morning nursing a severe hangover and asked my boss if I could leave at lunchtime as I was off to Turin. Fortunately, he let me have the time off work and I rushed home to pack my bags. I left a note for my mother to tell her I was off to Italy again and wasn't sure when I would be back. Just as

I headed over to Paul's house, my mother pulled up in her car. 'Where are you going?' she asked.

'Italy,' I replied. 'There's a note in the kitchen.'

She clearly didn't believe me, but as I had no time to explain things to her, she went home and read the note. I went round to Paul's home and played with his German Shepherd dog while Paul finished packing. We then took a train to Waterloo, a tube over to Heathrow, and we landed in Turin two hours later.

There were quite a few English fans on our plane, but certainly not enough to warrant the deployment of hundreds of riot police at Turin airport. As we went through passport control, a police dog started sniffing my leg - obviously the smell of Paul's dog had caught its attention. The police noticed this and bundled the two of us into a separate room while the dogs barked and snarled at our legs. The contents of our bags were unceremoniously dumped on the floor while the police kicked and poked at our clothes. After finding no drugs or weapons, they allowed us to re-pack our bags and proceed through the green channel.

Once safely through customs, we got chatting to an English lad who lived in Turin. He warned us that feelings were running high in the city, with many locals desperate for revenge over the death of 39 Juventus fans at the Heysel disaster in 1985. With nowhere to sleep and no tickets for the game, we certainly knew that we would have to be careful.

We jumped on a bus into the city centre and found a bar where a dozen or so English fans were drinking. We ordered a couple of cokes and topped up our glasses with duty free Bacardi. After speaking to these boys, it soon transpired that we would not be able to afford a hotel room, and in addition, most of the hotels confiscated your passport until such time as the hotel bill had been paid so it wasn't even possible to do a runner. We made our way to the train station and prepared to settle down for the night on a bench in the waiting room.

We were rudely awoken a couple of hours later by a group of police. We were ordered to stand up and frog marched to a waiting police van, inside which a few other English lads were already being held. None of us knew what was happening, but after the events in Rimini, a few of us thought we were being deported. We were driven at speed through Turin and found ourselves being delivered to a run down sports arena. There was a football pitch surrounded by a running track, all enclosed by a small bank of crumbling terracing.

We then spent an uncomfortable night trying to sleep on the hard concrete.

We gathered our senses in the early morning sunshine and had a brief look around our new found accommodation. Just around the corner was a small parade of shops. As I looked around the shops, an English lad pulled me over and asked if he could buy my copy of the *Evening Standard*. I let him have the paper and he was so impressed with my generosity that he stole me a huge bottle of red wine. We also bought bottles of wine, vodka and Bacardi and headed back to the makeshift campsite. The police refused to let us in with our supplies so we handed the alcohol to two of the lads who then walked around the perimeter of the camp and met us on the far side. They passed the bottles over the wall and returned to the main entrance empty handed, where the police were now happy to let them in. We spent the rest of the day, drinking, sunbathing and talking. Throughout the day, more English fans appeared as trains from Naples started arriving in the city.

That night, Argentina knocked Italy out of the World Cup in a penalty shoot out in Naples. Although we hated the Argentineans, we were as pleased as punch. After the way we had been treated by the Italian people, we were pleased that they were no longer in the tournament. In addition, we all felt we could beat the Argies in the final, if we could get past the Germans.

Shortly after the game had finished, pieces of rock started flying into the campsite. We grouped together and carefully strolled over to the perimeter fences. We could see hundreds of Italian Ultras down the street, their faces covered by black and white Juventus scarves. We tried to scale the fences, but they were just too high for enough of us to escape and confront the Italians. Seeing us, the Italians charged towards us, launching missiles as they did so. As the debris landed, we picked it up and returned fire.

Outside, the police turned up and chased the Italians away. We mobbed up again, picked up what weapons we could and headed to the far side of the campsite. Just over the fence, we could see a pile of rubble. A few of us jumped over, picked up as many pieces of rubble as we could and threw them back to our friends in the campsite. Meanwhile, another group of lads had broken into the groundsman's hut and had set light to the lawnmower. The fire and smoke added to the tense atmosphere.

A few minutes later, the Ultras appeared again. Armed with our array of weapons, we scaled the fence and ran into the Italians.

Once again, they ran for their lives. Our pursuit didn't last long, as the police turned up and baton charged us back into our complex. We stood behind the fence and aimed our weapons at the police and their cars. In return, they fired canister after canister of C.S gas. One canister landed in the dug out by the halfway line, half choking the lad who was sleeping on the bench, oblivious to the events going on all around him.

We picked up each cartridge and flung them back at the police. We also smashed up the contents of the groundsman's hut and smashed the dressing rooms. The terracing was broken up and more missiles were gathered to be thrown at the police. These clashes continued long into the night, until such time as the police stopped firing the canisters into the crowd. Once the situation calmed down, I feared the police would steam the camp and arrest or deport all of us. Fortunately, they now appeared to be very wary of us and wisely kept their distance.

On the morning of the game, the search for match tickets became our number one priority. The police refused to allow us to leave the immediate area of the campsite, which meant that we could not go into town or to the ground to try to buy tickets. Eventually, representatives of the FA turned up. We formed an orderly queue while we waited for news of the tickets. Rumours were circulating that the Germans had been given 40,000 tickets compared to our paltry allocation of 2,500, and when the news came it was not good. The FA only had a limited number of tickets priced in the most expensive category. These tickets would only be sold to members of the official England supporters club.

With the cost of membership and the tickets, I felt we were all being ripped off by the Football Association. The crowd voiced their anger and Graham Kelly was brought in. Behind a fence and a line of police, he addressed the crowd. He said the FA had done all they could, and at great expense, to secure extra tickets for us. We were told we should be grateful to the FA and the Italian authorities. These remarks were met by a stream of abuse.

'Why have the Krauts got 40,000 tickets?' asked a number of disgruntled fans.

Kelly replied, 'If you don't like it, you shouldn't have bothered coming. We don't want you here anyway.'

These comments infuriated everyone in the crowd who had spent hundreds of pounds to get there. All of us had been treated abysmally by everyone in Italy and now this was the gratitude we were receiving from the FA. Kelly scurried off into his office while the police battled in vain to calm the fans down.

I decided to try to break out of the campsite and head over to the ground in search of a tout. We saw a gap in the police line and charged through it, and fortunately we were not spotted. I felt wonderful as I walked through Turin, admiring the imposing Alpine mountain range in the distance. We stopped at a number of bars and enjoyed our new found freedom over a few cold beers. I started to appreciate that this is probably how fans of other countries were spending their days.

When we reached the Delli Alpi stadium, we stood in awe as we marvelled at the wonderful architecture of this new purpose built stadium. The car park was packed with thousands of German fans, all peacefully waiting by their cars or camper vans. We searched desperately for an English tout, but to no avail. Just as were about to give up and head to the train station, a German approached us and offered to sell us two tickets for just over the face value price. Although this meant that we would be sat with the Germans, we decided to buy the tickets and made our way back to the campsite via a few more bars.

We arrived back and sat around drinking and relaxing on the terraces. A camper van was parked nearby and the eerie sounds of Pink Floyd came from its speakers. The occupants of the van were smoking pot and generally chilling out. Another lad had a portable stereo and a tape of Winston Churchill's war time speeches was being loudly played. The promise to 'never surrender' and to 'fight them on the beaches' filled us with national pride, and increased our hatred of the Germans. As kick-off time approached we were really getting in the mood.

A convoy of buses took us to the stadium under heavy police escort. We only arrived about half an hour before kick-off and so we decided to make our way straight into the ground. As we thought, we found ourselves in the German end, sat at the front of the top tier. My concern at our seating arrangements eased when a mob of 30 or so Carlisle fans came and sat next to us. 'Any shit from these Krauts and we'll steam straight into them,' one of the Carlisle boys told me.

Our National Anthem was sung as loudly as we could and the German anthem was booed as loudly as possible. Well, it has to be done, doesn't it? As we booed their anthem, a few coins were thrown at us from the back of the stand. We all turned round to confront the Germans, but before we could move, the police pushed their way through the crowd and forced us to sit down.

We started to watch the game, a tight battle between two fully committed teams. In the 59th minute, Brehme took a free kick which deflected off the unfortunate Paul Parker and looped over the head of Peter Shilton. 1-0 to the Germans. We sat with our heads in our hands as all around us thousands of Germans celebrated the goal. Rather graciously, the German fan seated next to me offered to shake my hand. 'Fuck off,' I replied.

The Germans continued singing and shouting until the 80th minute when a long pass from Paul Parker was picked up by Lineker. He turned and shot past Illgner in the German goal. The ball hit the back of the net and thousands of English fans went crazy. All of us in the German end turned round to face the Germans and celebrated directly in front of them. The police came over and ordered us out of the German end. They then escorted us into the next block, where the bulk of the England fans were seated.

The game went into extra time where both teams had great chances to clinch victory. Neither team could score and so we had to face the dreaded penalty shoot out. We watched helplessly as Lineker, Beardsley and Platt all converted their spot kicks. Stuart Pearce then walked up and belted the ball towards the goal. Illgner managed to get his legs to it and prevented the ball from going in. When Thon converted his effort, our hopes lay at the feet of Chris Waddle. Unfortunately the pressure was too much for him and he struck the ball high over the bar.

The World Cup was over for England, but for the fans, we still had the small matter of getting home. Outside the ground, the police had arranged for buses to take us back to our campsite. When we arrived back, a number of fires were lit and rocks were thrown at the police. Attempts were being made to orchestrate another night of violence, but most of the England fans appeared to be too downhearted at the result of the match. More buses arrived to take us to the train station, so we gathered our belongings and joined the exodus. We arrived at the station to be met by hundreds of other England fans. They told us they had been involved in violent clashes with the Germans and a number of fans, both Germans and Italians, had been stabbed.

As we stood chatting in the station concourse, a flare was fired into the crowd. The Germans had arrived to bring the fight to us. Instantly, we dropped our bags and charged out to confront them. There was a brief fight before the Germans fled and the police baton charged us back into the station. Many of the fans had put up with this police brutality for four weeks and the general consensus amongst all of us was that the police were out of order. We had been attacked by the Germans and had acted in self-defence, and yet the Germans were allowed to leave the area while the police attacked us for having the bottle to defend ourselves. Enough was enough and we all decided to have one last go at the police. The chances were that we would just be deported now that England had been knocked out of the tournament, and the prospect of a free ticket home was very attractive to most of the fans as many of us were now skint.

As the police attacked us, many of us stood our ground. Unfortunately, it was never going to last and our brief show of solidarity did not work. Many of us took severe beatings. A train arrived and we were all forced onto it, despite the fact that none of us knew where it was going. A few hopefuls thought it was going to Bari as that was the location of the third place play-off between Italy and England.

After a while of travelling in the dark, I managed to nod off to sleep. When I awoke, none of the other lads in our compartment knew where we were or where we were heading. The other lads were Man City fans, but there was one lad on his own who had remained silent ever since he boarded the train. We asked him who he supported. Nervously, he admitted he was Dutch and had been to the game because he liked the English and hated the Germans. That was good enough for us and we befriended the Dutch lad, much to his relief.

Eventually, the train pulled to a stop at a station in the middle of nowhere. A few of us got off and bought some food and drink. We were somewhere in France and as the shop did not accept Italian lira, we had no alternative but to steal what we wanted. One of the boys went up to the train driver and asked where we were going. He was told him that he were heading for Paris. This news was greeted with sighs of relief amongst the lads in my compartment. The Mancs decided to empty the contents of their bag and make room for the goods they were planning on stealing in the French capital. Other fans soon had the same idea and a stream of lads walked up and down the train desperately trying to sell their clothes. Most of these clothes had been worn for three or four weeks, and were in need of a good wash, so very few sales were made.

The train made its way into Paris and as it did so, the fixtures and fittings were ripped out and thrown at passing traffic. Instead of slowing down to stop though, the train sped up and much to our dismay continued on through Paris and up towards Calais. When it arrived in Calais we were met by English and French police and were told to pay five pounds each for the cost of the ferry back to Dover. We all refused to pay, and as the police had no alternative plan they had no option but to allow us to board the ferry free of charge. As I went on board, the last thing I saw was our Dutch friend desperately trying to explain to the police that he was Dutch and had no desire to take a ferry to Dover. He obviously didn't like the English that much after all.

Ireland, 1990

LIKE MANY ENGLISHMEN, I have nothing against the vast majority of Irish people, both in the Republic of Ireland and in Ulster. However, the murderous activities of a minority of Irish people masquerading as freedom fighters tarnishes the good reputation of the many law abiding and decent Irish people. It is also common knowledge that many of the boys who regularly travel abroad to watch England play have extreme right wing political beliefs. For these reasons, any games between England and Ireland, particularly if played in Dublin, have the potential for serious disorder.

The close proximity of Dublin to England also means that thousands of young English lads can easily make the short trip. As a 19 year old, I was not mature enough to realise that not all Irish people were English hating terrorists, and I made the trip over to Dublin genuinely believing that everyone I met would be an IRA sympathiser.

Five of us decided to go over for the game, including one lad from Devon who we'd met in Italy. We were booked on the early morning flight from Gatwick to Dublin on the Tuesday and the game was due to be played on Wednesday afternoon. We arrived in Dublin in time for opening time, but our first task was to find bed and breakfast accommodation. The taxi driver took us to a street not far from the city centre where there was a wide selection of guest houses and hotels. We knocked on countless doors and received the same reply from every landlady. 'Sorry, fully booked up.'

One of the landladies was kind enough to advise to go to the tourist information office in O'Connell Street where they would phone around the various establishments until they found us a room. The girl in the tourist information office phoned a number of places, but the only place that would accommodate us was the youth hostel. We paid our deposit, took our directions and walked off to find the hostel. As it turned out, it wasn't far from the top of O'Connell Street.

As we reached the door, the manager confronted us. 'Are you English?' he asked.

49

When we confirmed that we were he told us he was fully booked up. 'That's fine, we've got a reservation.'

The news went down like a lead balloon, but as he had already accepted our booking over the telephone, he really had no alternative but to allow us to stay.

We checked in and went upstairs to the dormitory. The place stunk of sweat, but as it was so cheap we just decided to make do. We showered and changed and headed over to the pub opposite the hostel. We settled down in this pub and ordered some food and drink. Just after our arrival, a news bulletin came over the radio confirming that the British army had killed an IRA suspect in Belfast. The news was met with cheers from our camp, but our happiness was not shared by our jovial host. It was clear we were not welcome in this establishment and so we left and headed off into the city centre. Just round the corner from the pub, we spotted the local Sinn Fein offices. We made a mental note of its location and promised ourselves we would attack it later on.

The afternoon was spent moving from pub to pub in the centre of Dublin's fair city. There were different groups of English lads in each of the pubs and the conversations followed the usual lines. None of the English lads we met had tickets for the game and the rumours circulating amongst the English were that tickets would be very hard to come by. Old friends from Glasgow and Alghero were in Dublin and it was good to see each other again. An interesting story was also doing the rounds. Apparently, there was to be an IRA anti-extradition march in O'Connell Street after the game. If this was true, we were all determined to attack it.

We visited numerous pubs throughout the afternoon and by early evening we were all drunk. A dodgy looking Irish lad came over to us in Grafton Street. 'Do you want tickets for the game?' he asked.

Without saying a word to each other, we all knew we were going to rob him. 'Is it genuine - let's have a look,' one of us said.

He pulled the ticket from his back pocket and presented it to us. One of us punched him, one of us kicked him and the other three grabbed the ticket. In the midst of the melee, the ticket was ripped to pieces and the Irish lad managed to escape. Our search for tickets continued.

Our search naturally took us to more and more pubs. As we spoke to other English fans it was clear that there had been quite a few disturbances already that evening, although we had missed most of them. There didn't seem to be any mobs of Irish lads hanging around so I could only think that the English were fighting each other.

On the day of the game, we once again headed for O'Connell Street. There were gangs of touts trying to sell tickets, but the prices they wanted were well over the odds. We got chatting to one of the touts who advised us that he had a number of forgeries for sale. They were in the Irish end, but as they were forgeries he was selling them on the cheap. We took a gamble and decided to buy the tickets.

We spent the rest of the afternoon drinking in the centre of Dublin and decided to make our way over to the ground in good time. We felt that a few other English would buy these forged tickets and that, sooner rather than later, the police would get wise to the situation. We wanted to be in the ground before the turnstile operators were warned, so we boarded a dart train to Lansdowne Road.

I queued up at the gates and was relieved when the turnstile operator let me in after only taking a cursory look at the match ticket. All the other lads also made it in without any problems. We grouped up and found ourselves at the bottom of a large open terrace. It was virtually deserted as most of the Irish fans were still in the pubs, but there was a couple of hundred Irish fans stood at the back of the terrace. They instantly spotted we were English and began taunting us. 'You'll never beat the Irish!'

We didn't chant back at them but made gestures to them to come down and fight us. The police quickly became aware of this developing flash point and headed towards us. They kept us guarded while they decided what to do with us. The bulk of the English fans were to be seated in the stand to our left. Between the stand and the Irish end was a small pen of terracing which the police had obviously been hoping to keep empty. Our presence in the home end meant that they had no alternative but to house us in there.

There was still about 45 minutes to kick-off and the old stadium was now starting to fill up. The police were now aware that English fans were gaining entry to the Irish end by virtue of forged tickets and announcements were being made warning everyone that forged tickets were on sale. The English that had made it into the Irish end were swiftly spotted and escorted into our pen by the police. There were mobs from Aston Villa and Chelsea in amongst us, as well as a group of Belfast loyalists who supported Linfield.

When the players emerged for the kick-off, the atmosphere exploded. The Irish really made a lot of noise with their usual chants about our recent failure to beat them and their love for Molly Malone. The English replied with *Rule Britannia* and *God Save The Queen*.

The players lined up for the national anthems and the Irish stood to attention as their anthem was played. The English fans booed their anthem and waited for *God Save The Queen* to be played. When the Irish anthem ended, our players stood tall ready to sing our anthem. Nothing happened and all the players were looking at each other, wondering what was happening. Someone said something to the Irish players who ran off to warm up for the game. The English players were told something and then they too raced off to warm up for the game.

The English fans were furious. It turned out that the FA and the Irish FA had agreed not to play the English national anthem as they feared it could incite crowd trouble. We were told that the Irish anthem would not be played in the return game at Wembley the following year. This decision infuriated all of us and was a diabolical liberty. It had made the players look mugs as well, since no one had the decency to tell them what was happening beforehand. The English fans reacted in a typically violent way. Coins were launched at the Irish fans on the terracing to our left. Throughout the game, the English fans continually chanted the national anthem, as if making a point to the fools at the English and Irish Football Associations.

The game itself was very poor, as most games between these two countries usually are. The game ended 1-1. The group of English stood on the terracing were kept in the ground while the Irish fans left the area. I briefly spoke to some of the Belfast loyalists who confirmed that there was indeed an IRA march in Dublin that afternoon, hence their presence at the match.

We were still kept in the ground, but the English fans in the seats were allowed out. Once they were out on the streets, the clashes started. Looking out into the street below me, I could see hundreds of English charging up the roads, knocking over souvenir stalls, before picking them up and throwing them at the police and Irish fans. The Irish police appeared to be completely bewildered at this type of behaviour and didn't have a clue how to deal with it.

We couldn't wait to join our fellow countrymen out in the streets and when the police let us out of the ground, we rushed into the street. The Irish fans had dispersed, but we decided to walk back to the city centre and see if we could find any Irish mobs on the way. It was a very long and uneventful walk back to the city centre, but as we approached O'Connell Street, we walked straight into a running battle involving hundreds of people. The English were fighting the Irish, but these were not typical Irish football fans. I took a closer look and realised these were the Republican sympathisers who had gathered for the IRA march.

The running battles continued on the bridge over the River Liffey. The IRA meeting was taking place opposite the Post Office on O'Connell Street and the Republicans were hell bent on not allowing us on to O'Connell Street. At one stage, we forced the Irish back and made some progress up O'Connell Street. Suddenly, I could see thousands of IRA supporters in the street. They saw us and let off a huge roar. They charged into us and chased us back across the bridge. I continued running and turned round to be confronted by dozens of mean looking Republicans still desperately trying to catch me. I realised there was only me and another lad and wondered where all the other English fans had gone. The chase continued and at one stage I thought I could run no more. I looked around, and to my horror I was still being chased. Suddenly, I had visions of being tortured by balaclava wearing terrorists armed with baseball bats. These nightmares forced me to keep on running, and eventually I turned round to see the Irish lads had given up their pursuit.

The lad I was with turned out to be a Wigan fan. I told him that I would have to go back to where I had come from as I was staying at the other end of O'Connell Street. He wished me good luck and wandered off in search of his ferry. I cautiously made my way back in the direction of the hostel. The streets were full of Irish fans chanting, 'You'll never beat the Irish!', and it felt like every pair of eyes was staring through me, but with hindsight, this was probably just paranoia on my part.

I reached the bridge over the Liffey only to be met by the sight of hundreds of Republicans in O'Connell Street directly opposite. I decided to turn right and walked down a street parallel to the river. After a while, I came across a mob of English fans who were mobbing up and planning on attacking the IRA sympathisers from a side street just off O'Connell Street. I stuck with these boys as we walked through the narrow side streets. As we neared O'Connell Street, a large roar sounded and we rushed towards the main street. It appeared that we had taken them by surprise and the people nearest to us were attacked. Again, sheer numbers forced us to retreat. Throughout these clashes that had taken place in and around O'Connell Street, the police had been useless. As the battles continued however, riot police were drafted in and they were only too happy to fight with the English and also with the Republicans.

Our mob stayed in the back streets before regrouping and attacking O'Connell Street once again. Our intention was to seize O'Connell Street back from the IRA. A break away mob of Republicans came looking for us, but without the numbers they suffered a terrible defeat. With nowhere to run to, they were caught and plenty of them were seriously injured. One of them was trapped in a doorway where he was kicked unconscious. He was then picked up and thrown threw a shop window. This mob of IRA sympathisers continued to get a severe beating until the riot police arrived and dispersed us.

We broke away from the police and continued walking up the side streets in an attempt to find a way back onto O'Connell Street. After some time we found a way and charged down the street towards the IRA supporters, kicking and punching anyone who stood in our way. Before we could reach the bulk of the Provos, we were confronted by a thick line of riot police who baton charged us back down the side streets.

Our mob was forced to split up into different groups, all closely pursued by riot police. Their plan was to keep us moving away from O'Connell Street. If you stood still or tried to walk away, you were viciously assaulted. We were pushed towards a bus station where the majority of people boarded buses to take them back to the ferry port. As I had a flight ticket I didn't want to join these buses and managed to break away.

I now found myself alone again on the streets of Dublin where I knew there were hundreds of IRA supporters searching for Englishmen. I kept my wits about me and headed back to Grafton Street. I sat in a burger bar for an hour or so, hoping the crowds would die down. I eventually emerged to discover that O'Connell Street was no longer packed with IRA supporters. I started to walk towards O'Connell Street, but as I reached the top of the street, I noticed large groups of teenagers on the look out for English stragglers.

I felt sure they would deduce I was English and so I stood in a telephone box while I thought about my next move. About five or six English lads came out of a hotel carrying their luggage, searching for a taxi. The Irish teenagers spotted them and charged across the road to confront them. The English guys dropped their luggage and steamed straight into their assailants.

As the two gangs set about each other, I spotted a taxi in the street trying to weave its way through the scuffle. I raced over and opened the back door. 'You'll have to get one from the rank,' shouted the driver as I slumped on the back seat. 'Fuck the rank, just drive.'

Alerted by the urgency in my voice, the driver obliged and drove away from the fight. It was only a short ride and in no time at all I was back in the safety of the youth hostel. The sound of a television could be heard in one of the communal rooms and so I went in there to see if the trouble was on the news. Sure enough, the news was on and the reporter was discussing the events that had taken place in the city centre that evening. The other people staying in the hostel listened attentively to the news report and then started to slag off all the English fans for their outrageous behaviour. Judging by their appearance, these people didn't even have the decency to keep themselves clean, but were quite happy to slag off English people after hearing a biased report on the news. I couldn't be bothered to argue and left them to it. I went upstairs, had a shower, and retired to my bed.

A little while later, I was awoken by the sound of the other lads returning home. As they entered the dormitory, their appearance and their smell indicated that they had all been drinking. We had got split up earlier on in the evening when it first kicked off on the bridge at the bottom of O'Connell Street. While I was running for my life in fear of being taken hostage by a gang of Provos, they had found a friendly pub and had stayed in there, drinking and chatting, until the streets quietened down. One of the lads had heard a dubious story that an English fan had been killed at some point in the evening. He didn't know the exact circumstances, but was so sure the story was true, he had told the taxi driver who in turn told every other taxi driver in Dublin over his walkie-talkie.

The following morning, we went off to a pub in O'Connell Street for lunch and a livener before hiring a cab to take us back to the airport. The pub was packed with England fans, many of whom we knew. We all sat about, reading the papers, drinking, and taking the piss out of each other. Another English lad entered the pub and came over to our table. He introduced himself as a Stoke fan and then asked us if we had heard about the England fan who had been taken away and shot dead by the IRA last night.

'No, who told you that?', we asked.

'A taxi driver,' he replied.

The Irish papers roundly condemned the English fans for our behaviour in Dublin after the game, and to be fair, I have to say, the violence was amongst the most fierce I have ever witnessed. However, it is easy to shift all the blame onto the English fans as we are obvious scapegoats and everyone will be only too happy to sit back and accept it. A few questions should be asked before the English fans accept full responsibility though. Whose idea was it to organise an anti-extradition march in the centre of Dublin, timed to coincide with the arrival of thousands of England fans from Lansdowne Road? This was surely down to Gerry Adams and his cronies within Sinn Fein or the IRA, if you are still gullible enough to believe that they are two separate organisations. Tony Blair obviously is, but most England fans know the truth. Their motives are obvious. The IRA propaganda machine will spout the usual rubbish about how it was a peaceful gathering until it was ambushed by far right extremists from England. The sad thing is, this tissue of lies will be believed by millions of *Guardian* reading do gooders back home in England.

The Dublin police must have approved the timing and location of the meeting well in advance, yet they did nothing to prevent thousands of England fans from walking towards the march. Did they think we were going to offer the hand of friendship to the people responsible for killing and maiming hundreds of Englishmen over the years? Did the chants of 'No surrender to the IRA!', sung throughout our time in Dublin, not indicate that we were all fiercely opposed to the Republican movement? The presence of well known hard-line loyalists from Belfast within the England crowd might have given the game away if the Irish police had used just a little bit of common sense.

But instead of using the powers granted to them, they allowed the skirmishes to start and only acted some time later when riot police were deployed in the city. Surely, a share of the blame should lie with them too.

I am personally proud of the way the England fans attacked the IRA and its cowardly supporters that night. England and

56

Northern Ireland would be a much safer place if known IRA men were attacked each time they took to the streets. In London, the IRA organise at least two marches a year, while the police have to waste their time and money ensuring the IRA are not attacked by angry Londoners. Perhaps it is this feeble attitude of the Government towards terrorism that instils so much anger amongst many English fans. When an opportunity to strike at the heart of the IRA arises, we at least tried to take their opportunity. We may not have succeeded as well as we would have liked, but at least we showed the IRA that some English people will never surrender.

Wales, 1991

In February, 1991, England arranged to play a friendly against Cameroon at Wembley, but I had no interest in attending this game. Generally speaking, I can't stand going to Wembley. Normally, it takes ages to get there, there are very few decent pubs, you get ripped off at the ground, the atmosphere is poor, and the football is usually dire.

On the same night as the Cameroon game, England had also arranged to play Wales at the Vetch Field in Swansea, in a friendly 'B' international. This game appealed to me as it was the first time England had played in Wales for a number of years. The Welsh football fans hate the English with a vengeance. Both Cardiff and Swansea, and to a lesser extent, Wrexham, have naughty mobs, although in my experience, most of the hooligans that follow Wales come from Cardiff. As the game was to be played in Swansea, I didn't feel any Cardiff fans would turn up because of the intense rivalry between themselves and Swansea. This would leave us with just the Swansea fans to contend with.

An Arsenal fan we met in Alghero was organising a coach trip to the game and so one of my other mates, who also goes to Arsenal, met up with him and paid our deposit for the trip. The coach was leaving North London early on the morning of the game.

We arrived at the pick up point to be confronted by about 40 faces from Millwall, Arsenal and Chelsea. Most of the faces were familiar to me, either from Dublin or Italy, and we joined the coach in high spirits. As we set off west out of London, the smell of drugs and alcohol already filled the coach. A few of the boys had brought some video tapes to keep us amused on the long journey. There were a couple of pornographic films, the film *Scum*, with Ray Winstone, and the *Panorama* documentary about Millwall and Harry The Dog. Unfortunately, this was only shown briefly as the Chelsea and Arsenal fans demanded it be turned off.

After a brief stop at Slough to pick up a few Chelsea fans, we headed towards the Severn Bridge and could see the weather drastically changing as we drove further away from London. When we had left London it was a sunny, winter's morning, with not a cloud in the sky. However, as we approached Wales there was snow falling and the temperature was dropping below zero. None of us had come prepared for this sort of weather.

Before crossing into enemy territory, we decided to stop off for a drink and pulled off the motorway and into the small town of Avonmouth. We quickly found a pub with a pool table and jukebox and decided to settle down in here for the afternoon to get pissed up before arriving in Swansea. The landlady was not expecting 40 thirsty Londoners to turn up in her seedy back street pub in the sleepy town of Avonmouth and looked quite concerned at first. However, we all behaved ourselves and certainly helped to increase her profits.

Once fully lubricated, we continued our journey, crossing over the Severn bridge into Wales. In no time at all, we were in Swansea, driving around looking to find somewhere to park the coach. Eventually, the driver dropped us off on the main road, not far from the prison, and told us to return at 11.00 for the return journey back to London. This was kind of him as it meant we would have time to go into Swansea after the game for a drink.

We had about an hour to go to kick-off and so we decided to head for a pub near the ground. There were a few Welsh fans inside, but as we strolled in they finished their beers and left. There were no incidents in the pub, and we had a few beers and then left for the match, sticking together just in case of an ambush. Nothing happened on the way to the ground and it looked like nothing was going to happen.

The fact that the game was just a 'B' international meant that the game had not captured the imagination of the local lads. I had been certain that as they were playing England, a few of their boys would have turned out. Still, their failure to show meant that the trip was more of a beano than anything else.

We reached the ground and decided against standing in the away end. Quite a few England fans had turned up, including many from Wolverhampton who were there to cheer on their hero, Steve Bull. We decided to sit down in the main stand, right in the corner near the home end. If Wales did have a mob, they could not fail to notice 40 pissed up England fans sat in their seats.

The game kicked off and we settled down to watch it. By now, it was so cold you could not sit down comfortably for any length of time, and as we all had the taste for beer, it was obvious that we were not going to watch the full 90 minutes.

Well before the end of the match, we decided to leave and head into the town centre to look for some action. After a short walk, we found ourselves in a street with numerous pubs. The streets themselves were fairly deserted - after all it was a freezing cold night - but one pub looked particularly lively. There were a number of girls drinking in there and there was also a karaoke machine. We strolled into this pub and as more and more of us walked over to the bar, the bouncers, who had been stood in the far corner of the pub, came over to us. 'Sorry lads, no trainers'.

'Okay then,' replied one of the Chelsea lads. 'Fucking kick us out'.

The bouncers backed down and had no choice but to let us take over the bar. The jovial atmosphere in the pub changed to one of apprehension as the locals realised we were all English. A few got up to leave, while the others continued drinking, making sure they kept their heads down and avoiding all eye contact with any of the English lads.

They needn't have worried. We were not the sort of fans to smash a pub up just for the sake of it. We were quite happy drinking and chatting amongst ourselves. This was what was happening until one of the locals decided to impress his girlfriend with his impersonation of Welsh heart throb, Tom Jones. He grabbed the microphone and stood up to sing *The Green, Green Grass Of Home*.

Before he could finish the first line of the song, another of the Chelsea boys had grabbed him by the neck. The bouncers charged over and pulled the Chelsea fan from the singing Welshman. This heavy handed action by the bouncers prompted the other Chelsea fans to confront the bouncers. It looked like a full scale bar brawl was about to erupt, but the bar staff warned us that they had pressed the panic button which meant that the police were on their way. We all decided to leave before their arrival and went off to find another pub.

The flashpoint in the pub meant that we were all buzzing and well up for it. As we walked along the street, we noticed three or four lads on the other side of the street. A couple of boys from our group crossed the road. 'Come on Swansea!' they yelled, before charging towards them.

'We're English,' they replied, which was enough to stop our two boys in their tracks.

'Where are you from then?'

'Swindon,' was the answer given.

The two boys thought about it for a moment and one said, 'That's near enough to Wales for me,' and continued towards the poor Swindon fans, who decided enough was enough and ran off to safety. Luckily the two lads gave up the chase almost immediately. They had been a bit out of order, but as the Swindon boys escaped without getting hurt, we all saw the funny side of it.

We continued heading up this street and could hear the sound of disco music blaring out from a night club. We decided to try to get into the night club, but we knew our chances of being allowed in were very slim. I couldn't see any bouncers letting 40 pissed up, aggressive Englishmen into a night club in the middle of Swansea on the night England had played Wales. Still, we gave it a go and weren't too surprised when the bouncers refused us admission on the grounds that we were all wearing trainers.

Just inside the door, a couple of Welsh lads laughed when they heard the bouncers turning us away. They weren't laughing for long though. One of the Chelsea fans pulled out a flare gun and aimed it directly at the bouncers. They ducked for cover as the flare was launched straight into the club, causing much panic amongst the revellers. Once the flare had been launched, we steamed into the bouncers, but there were too many of us to get through the doors.

Suddenly, a bar stool came flying out of the window from inside the club, closely followed by a number of bottles and glasses. All these missiles were thrown back into the club while a couple of us tried to pick up a motorbike that was parked outside, in an effort to launch that through the window too. Unfortunately, it proved to be too heavy. The bouncers managed to lock the doors and the clubbers refused to bring the fight out on to the street. As the police sirens grew louder we decided it was time to make our exit, so the 40 of us walked away, hoping we wouldn't be spotted by the police.

The police did manage to find us but instead of stopping us or questioning us, they just decided to follow us instead. A few of the Chelsea lads managed to break away and ran down a side street in an effort to escape the attention of the police. We were prevented from joining them and another police van was dispatched to locate the rogue Chelsea element. We ended up being escorted to our coach where we waited for the Chelsea fans to rejoin us.

They failed to turn up and we suspected they had been arrested. We asked the coach driver to drive around the town to see if we could find them, but when that failed, we drove to the police station to see if they'd been arrested. The police confirmed that they had indeed been detained, but it was clear that the police did not want to hold them in custody. After careful negotiations, the police agreed to release the Chelsea fans on the condition that they would give our coach a police escort out of Swansea.

We agreed to the terms of this 'peace treaty' and set off out of Swansea, closely followed by the South Wales police. They continued following us all the way to the Severn Bridge, where they left us and returned to Swansea. Shortly after entering England again, it was decided to make a refreshment stop and we pulled over into a service station. Cans of drink and bags of crisps were the order of the day, but instead of paying for the goods, everyone walked out and sat back down on the coach. The sales assistant was helpless to prevent the thieving and watched in horror as we continued on our journey along the M4.

We were dropped off back in North London and gave the coach driver a generous trip. He had put up with drink, drugs and pornographic films on the journey to and from Wales, had been forced to drive around Swansea until we could secure the release of prisoners, and had been witness to highway robbery. At all times he genuinely appeared to be enjoying the escapades. It certainly beat taking a group of pensioners to Windsor Castle for the day anyway.

Kilburn, 1991

IN MARCH, 1991, just six weeks after the trip to Swansea, England faced the Republic Of Ireland at Wembley in a qualifying match for the 1992 European Championships to be held in Sweden. With so many Irish people living in England, there were bound to be thousands of Irish fans at Wembley and the chances of segregating the rival fans successfully would be very slim indeed.

I was still fuming about the failure of the Irish Football Association to play our national anthem at the game in Dublin earlier on in the season. We had been advised that the English FA would refuse to play the Irish national anthem, but I couldn't see this happening. The events in and around O'Connell Street were also still fresh in my mind and I felt I had a score to settle with the Irish, and in particular, the supporters of the IRA.

Once again, I didn't have a ticket for the match, but this did not concern me as I made my way into London on the morning of the game. We went for a drink in Shakespeare's, outside Victoria Station, and although it was still early, there was already a large mob of English boys drinking in the pub. I recognised the accents as being from the North East and when one of the lads came over to the bar, I asked him who they were. When he said they were Boro fans, I asked if he knew Nigel, our friend from Alghero. The lad knew him all right, and said he was sat over in the far corner. I went over to join him and spent the next few hours drinking with these boys.

After a while, we decided to make our way into the West End. A few of the Boro lads wanted to have a look at the shops in Old Bond Street so we arranged to meet up in The Hog In The Pound, a pub opposite the tube station. Just as we were leaving, a mob of Blues came into the pub. I recognised a few of them from our previous trips to Glasgow and Sardinia. We had a brief chat and I told them we were going to the pub in Bond Street. They said they would have a drink in here and then meet us at Bond Street a little later.

When we arrived at Bond Street, The Hog In The Pound was packed with the usual faces from Arsenal, Millwall and Chelsea, along with the mob from Villa that we knew from Alghero and Dublin.

63

I spoke to the Villa lads and said that I had met some Blues earlier on at Victoria and invited them to this pub. I knew that the rivalry between these mobs was so intense that they would not socialise under any circumstances. I didn't want any trouble between the two mobs as I got on fairly well with both of them, but the Villa fans were in no mood to welcome the Blues and I feared the worst.

The Villa fans were drinking in the downstairs bar so I started drinking upstairs, by the front door with a few of the Londoners. When the Blues turned up, we told them that a few Villa were drinking downstairs and that none of us wanted to find ourselves in the middle of a domestic dispute. The Blues were quite eager to go straight down the stairs and attack their rivals, but fortunately, they listened to what we had to say and agreed to drink elsewhere.

By mid afternoon, the pub was packed with some notorious faces from some of the top firms in the country. One of the boys decided to break into the cigarette machine and started thieving its contents. With hundreds of cigarettes stuffed down his shirt, he took his beer and started drinking outside. The bar staff quickly realised the cigarette machine had been broken into and called the police. They turned up shortly afterwards and couldn't help but notice the lad outside the pub with hundreds of cigarettes hanging out of his clothing.

The bar staff started to get a bit of stick for being grasses and the police decided to keep an eye on the pub. We decided enough was enough and left the West End to head for Kilburn. For many years, Kilburn has been the focal point of the large Irish community in London and we knew that many Irish fans would be drinking in the numerous pubs in the area. The Chelsea lad responsible for the flare gun attack on the Swansea night club was with us and once again he was carrying his favourite weapon. A few of the other boys were from North London and had told us about a pub which had a reputation for being staunchly IRA, with collection tins on the bar and regular events being held to raise funds for the cause. The Chelsea fan said that we must find this pub and attack it, an idea that went down particularly well with the rest of us.

We left The Hog In The Pound and joined a tube to take us to Kilburn. There was about 150 of us, including a few of the Belfast loyalists we had met in Dublin, and we were all carrying bottles or glasses. When the tube stopped at Kilburn, we got off and walked out on to the High Road. Opposite the tube station was a pub packed with Irish fans, and most of us wanted to attack them, but the Chelsea lads reminded us of our reason for being there.

There were no police in the area and after a short walk, we saw the pub we were looking for on our left. It was also packed with Irish fans, but without hesitation the Chelsea lads charged across the road, smashed the windows, and let off the flares in the pub. The rest of us quickly followed and threw everything we had. A lot of the Irish cowered under tables or behind the bar, but quite a few returned the missiles and some even made an effort to come out and confront us.

As they did so, a number of small scale fights broke out. One of the Irish lads had picked up a shopping trolley and was smashing it over the head of one of our boys, who himself was fighting another Irish lad. I spotted this attack and moved over to hit the Irish lad. It was a terrible punch and only just managed to connect with his head. The Irish lad didn't appear to feel any pain, but I certainly did as I felt a bone in my hand break. I backed off and noticed that the English were still throwing missiles into the pub. I picked up a bottle and tried to throw it, but with my broken hand, I didn't have the strength to launch it.

Next door to the pub was a shop with a rack of shoes on display outside. We had run out of missiles so were now reduced to throwing shoes into the bar. Unlike the bottles and glasses, the shoes were not thrown back at us by the Irish, so I can only assume that they thought we had given up attacking them and were now dishing out presents.

The fighting outside this pub stopped and so we continued on down the High Road. We approached another pub and helped ourselves to a skip full of rubble that was conveniently situated just outside. The pub full of Irish fans was soon on the receiving end of another ferocious assault. I must have looked a pathetic sight as I threw bottles under arm with my left hand. I could have sworn I saw the Irish laughing at my pathetic attempts at acting the big tough hooligan. I was never very good at it at the best of times, anyway.

One of the lads did a flying kick at the window of the pub and although he succeeded in smashing it, he couldn't get his leg out again. The Irish spotted his foot on the inside of the window and grabbed hold of it, desperately trying to drag him into the pub. He found himself the subject of a tug of war as we all desperately tried to pull him to safety. Fortunately we succeeded, because I wouldn't have fancied his chances of survival if the Irish had managed to pull him into the pub.

By now, the police were rushing down the High Road in an effort to reach us before we could cause anymore destruction. We soon found ourselves in the tube station, surrounded by police determined to get us out of Kilburn. As we stood at the top of the escalators, a policeman was stood in front of us, with his back towards us. One of the English lads kicked him in the back, sending the policeman stumbling down the steps. When we reached the bottom of the escalators, he was waiting for us and arrested the culprit. The lad was later charged with assaulting a police officer and with affray, but the case was thrown out of court due to lack of evidence.

We boarded the tube and headed to Wembley after a brief stop in Hampstead. By now, my hand was swelling up and turning blue, but I decided to delay going to hospital until I got home. I had purchased a ticket from one of the Arsenal boys in The Hog In The Pound and certainly didn't want to miss the game.

As I expected, the Irish anthem was indeed played before the game. Although I was furious, most of the England fans did not understand the significance as most had not been present in Dublin and the snub had not been widely reported in the English media. To make things worse, England once again failed to beat the Irish.

I went home tired and in pain, and went to the local hospital to get my hand checked out. I told the consultant I had broken it in a fight earlier on that day and as I was waiting for the results of the x-ray, the police turned up. They told me that there had been a fight in one of the pubs in town in which the victim had sustained a broken jaw. They wanted to take me down to the station to help them with their enquiries. Luckily, I had retained my match ticket and managed to convince them that I had been at Wembley at the time of the attack.

Poland, 1991

IN NOVEMBER, 1991, England faced Poland in a yet another vital match between the two countries. In 1973, we had to beat Poland to qualify for the 1974 World Cup in Germany. In 1986 we had to beat Poland in the World Cup and in 1989 we had to avoid defeat to guarantee qualification for the 1990 World Cup. The importance of these games and the fact that the Poles always made life difficult for England meant that something of a sporting rivalry had developed between the two nations. Come 1991 and once again we had to avoid defeat to ensure we qualified for a prestigious tournament, this time the 1992 European Championships to be held the following summer in Sweden.

The Poles were also attracting attention for the amount of violence that took place between rival fans in their own domestic league, and these rivalries and disputes were often settled at the big international games. A number of my friends had attended the game in Poland in 1989 and had made it clear that Poland was the place to go for football violence. The game that year had taken place in Katowice, a tough mining community in the heart of the Krakow region of Poland. The Poles were fighting each other all night and when they couldn't fight each other, they were more than happy to take on the English. The cost of accommodation, food, and drink was ridiculously cheap. All in all, it sounded like the perfect trip.

In 1991, the game was to take place in Poznan, a railway town half way between Berlin and Warsaw. After listening to all the stories from 1989, I was determined to make the trip and was pleased to hear that our friend from Arsenal was organising another trip. When details of the trip started to emerge, my excitement hit fever pitch. The plan was to fly to Berlin on Monday the 11th of November (a fine date to be visiting Germany), and after a day spent at leisure in Berlin, we would catch a train to Poznan on Tuesday, arriving in plenty of time for the game the following evening. Wednesday would be spent in Poznan preparing for the game that night and on

Thursday we would catch a train back to Berlin before flying back to Heathrow. The trip sounded perfect and I booked my flight ticket.

We arrived at Heathrow and discovered there were about 20 lads in our party. As usual, most of the boys were Arsenal, Chelsea and Millwall, although there were also a couple of Queens Park Rangers fans and a few Middlesborough fans. There were two flights to Berlin that afternoon, and as some of us were on the first flight with the others following on the second flight an hour later, we arranged to meet in the airport bar in Berlin.

Our flight arrived in Berlin and we wasted no time in finding the bar. We then settled down to enjoy some German beer while we waited for the other flight to land. As it turned out, that flight was delayed by a couple of hours, but time seemed to pass by as we chatted amongst ourselves and slowly got drunk. When the others arrived, we had a few more beers, and then took the bus into the city centre.

As we approached the city centre, our bus was overtaken by a convoy of police vans. Fortunately, the bus appeared to be heading in the same direction as the police and we continued to follow the blue lights. Eventually we turned a corner to see the police vans had come to a halt outside a bar. We pressed the emergency alarms and jumped off the bus to see what was happening. There were large groups of English fans outside the bar and some of them told us what had happened.

They said that the English had all been drinking and getting on with each other okay. The German staff in the bar were friendly and were happy to serve the thirsty English customers until a group of Man City fans sitting at the bar spotted the till had been left open. One of them tried to rob the takings, but was spotted by one of the staff. As a result of the attempted theft, the Germans decided to close the bar and asked the English to leave. A few Chelsea boys got the hump with the thieving City fans, accusing them of being out of order. The bar had been friendly and welcoming, but as a result of their petty thieving habits all the English now had to leave. What happened next wasn't clear, but the police turned up and arrested a couple of Chelsea fans. The City fans went off on their own and the rest of us made our way into the city centre.

We went round a few bars, but my initial impressions of Berlin was that it was a very dangerous place to be. Everywhere you went, there were small gangs of shady looking Turks and Africans loitering around. I had heard that these immigrants were often attacked by rival gangs of neo-Nazi skinheads in Berlin and other large cities throughout Germany. In response to these attacks, many immigrants carried knives with them and were quite prepared to use them.

We found ourselves in a bar next to a train station and settled down to continue drinking. We had no accommodation booked so the plan was to stay in this bar as long as possible and then catch an early morning train to Poznan. Most of us were sat on bench seats under the window, but two or three of the lads were sat at the bar. As we were sitting and drinking, a couple of Turkish lads came over to us. They didn't speak English, but appeared to be trying to sell us something. We just ignored them and they left us and walked over to our friends at the bar. I kept an eye on the two Turks, my instincts telling me there was something not quite right about them.

I saw them approach the lads at the bar and exchange pleasantries. Something untoward was obviously said and one of the Turks took offence. In an instant, he pulled a huge knife from his jacket pocket and slashed one of the lads above his ear and down the side of his cheek. The Turk then pulled the knife on the other lad, who at the same time jumped off his stool and hit the Turk with his glass. The knife penetrated his jacket, jumper and shirt, but fortunately the blade did not reach his skin. Once we were all aware of what was happening, we jumped up and went for the two Turks.

The knifeman was alert to the danger and managed to run out of the door. His companion though did not seem to realise what was happening and was still stood there with a cigarette hanging from the side of his mouth. One of our lads threw a punch which connected cleanly with the Turk's jaw. He crashed to the floor, unconscious, but with the cigarette still glued to his lips. We jumped over the prostrate Turk and ran after his mate. He was chased down the street, but managed to make good his escape. A German who just happened to be in the wrong place at the wrong time was not so lucky. He had C.S gas sprayed in his face. We returned to the pub to find the place surrounded by German police, with the other Turk still unconscious on the floor. The cigarette was still smoking.

The police rounded us up, arrested the lad who had sprayed the German with gas, and put the rest of us on a train. After a short journey, they told us to get off and we found ourselves on the concourse of a huge empty train station. We had a look outside but the streets were deserted. All we could see were tower blocks covered in graffiti. We were in East Berlin and, though only a short trip from where we had come from, it felt like we had travelled back in time.

Miraculously, we discovered that a train was going to Poznan shortly and so we waited for the train to depart. The train turned up and we boarded the Warsaw Express which went via Poznan. I fell asleep, but was awoken a few hours later by the sight of Polish customs officers. We were ordered off the train and asked to show our visas before the train could continue across the border. The customs officers checked each visa meticulously and ordered us to complete a form giving details of how much money we were importing into Poland. All this took some time, so we decided to leave the station to see if anything was open. It was only a small border town and at this time of the night the town square was deserted. We spotted what looked like a small convenience store. It was the middle of the night and naturally the shop was closed. However, after banging on the windows for a few minutes, an Indian looked out from an upstairs window. Realising there was a chance to make some money, he got dressed and rushed down to open the shop. He probably took more money in those ten minutes than he had all week. He certainly looked pleased with himself.

Armed with our goodies, we boarded the train for the final part of our outward journey. We arrived in Poznan and left the station in search of a taxi rank. We were staying in the Orbis Hotel and four or five taxi drivers were only too happy to take us there. Our taxi driver was fairly friendly and when we pulled up at the hotel, we willingly paid the fare. The other lads were all arguing with their drivers and it turned out that they were asking considerably more for the fare than our driver had charged. Their attempts at blatantly ripping us off backfired though when we refused to pay them. If they had all been like our driver, they would have made a tidy sum of money, but their greed cost them dearly.

We checked into our hotel, a smart, business orientated hotel, clearly suited to German businessmen. On this occasion, however, the hotel had been taken over by England fans. The hotel bar was doing a roaring trade and the cheap Polish beer was going down very well.

After a few beers we decided to take a stroll round the town. It was a drab and dreary place, and for some reason I imagined it would be like a ghost town, with very few people around. It was not like this at all though, and most shops and bars appeared to be fairly busy. There were certainly no long queues for loaves of bread. The boys who had visited Poland in 1989, before the Iron Curtain was torn down, couldn't believe the change in the economic climate.

On our travels, we came across a gun shop, a sex shop and a bar that served Heineken export on draught. The gun shop was our first stop and there were plenty of nasty looking weapons openly on sale. The open availability of these weapons prompted us to believe that the Polish fans would be tooled up. We didn't want to be at a disadvantage so a few of the boys purchased some new toys. The sex shop was our second port of call. There were a few English lads already in the shop marvelling at all the goodies. A tall, good looking, Polish girl entered the shop, and after a brief conversation, the sales assistant handed her a large carrier bag full of sex aids. As she left the shop, we all thought what a lucky bugger her husband was.

We made our way to the Heineken Bar where we bumped into old friends from Villa and Oldham. A pleasant day was then spent drinking. Occasionally, young Polish fans would approach us and try to exchange football scarves. They seemed very surprised that none of the English fans wore scarves or hats. The England national shirt appeared to be designed by Stone Island. The young Polish fans were decades behind in the fashion stakes, with their boys fully kitted out in skinhead regalia. The rise of the casual scene was still some time off in Poland.

That night, we were all the worse for wear. The cheap vodka was like firewater and the vodka and lager had been flowing all day. We went from bar to bar, but there were no gangs of Polish skinheads out on the town. We found ourselves drinking with different groups of fans. We were in one bar when we were approached by a gang of Northerners. They claimed they had been in a brothel and bumped into a certain former England star now working in the media. He wasn't too pleased to see them, but they were determined to expose him as a dirty pervert. If he was a dirty pervert for being in a brothel, I wondered how these Northerners would categorise themselves. Mind you, if it wasn't for his family, I'd gladly name and shame in.

The town was fairly quiet, so we returned to our hotel where we had been told that entertainment was provided every night. The entertainment appeared to consist of a very poor band, miming to old Abba hits, a local man who advertised himself as 'the rubber man', and hundreds of prostitutes plying their trade at the hotel bar. Very few of these girls spoke English, although it has to be said, many of them were stunning. The girl we had met in the sex shop earlier on in the day was at the bar, no doubt hoping her earlier investment would reap dividends.

We were told that there was a decent night club on the edge of town, so about 20 of us jumped in taxis and went in search of it. When we got there, the club had two rooms. One was full of pool tables and the other had a disco with a tiny dance floor. We went into the pool room and started knocking a few balls around. There were a few England fans already in the bar, but my first impressions of these lads was not good. It turned out they were Spurs fans and their general aloofness and the fact that they supported Tottenham was enough to wind all of us up. After a brief argument, they left the bar.

We played pool for a while longer and then decided to join the disco. The bouncers refused to let us in and so we surged past them and forced our way into the bar. The disco was empty and all our efforts to gain entry appeared to have been for nothing. We decided to return to our hotel, and fortunately our taxis were still waiting outside, but just as we left the car park, a load of police cars raced in. Unbeknown to us, the bouncers had called the police but they had turned up too late. We ordered the drivers to leave, but unfortunately the police spotted us and followed us back to our hotel.

When the taxis pulled into the car park outside the hotel, the police were right behind and jumped out to confront us. We weren't hanging around and ran off into the foyer. The police followed us and were quite happy to use their batons on anyone who stood in their way. We managed to get in the lifts before the police could catch up with us and completed our successful escape. Two of the lads weren't so lucky and were arrested the following morning. Fortunately, they were released without charge before the game.

On the Wednesday morning, we met up in the hotel bar. A few English had already been out and about and had noticed quite a few Poland fans were now converging on the town. As there was no action in the hotel bar we decided to make our way into the town centre. A few of the lads were too lazy to walk and jumped in cabs, but we decided to walk, just in case we bumped into any Poles. After an uneventful walk, we made it to the Heineken Bar where we had arranged to meet the other lads. They were not there and despite taking cabs to the bar, they didn't turn up for another 30 minutes. I thought the cabs may have taken them on a mystery tour, but it turned out that as they were driving through the town, they noticed a mob of skinheads. They ordered the cabs to drop them off and they charged at the skinheads. The Poles stood their ground and there was a brief toe to toe battle. The English were on top and eventually the Poles were forced to retreat. The skinheads made good their escape on a passing tram, and as the tram passed the English, they let rip with a volley of verbal abuse. Further down the line, the tram came to a halt at a red light. The English ran down, forced the doors open and sprayed the Poles with C.S. gas. They left the Poles screaming in pain and came to meet us in the bar, very pleased with themselves.

We spent the rest of the day drinking without any further problems. With kick-off rapidly approaching, we jumped in taxis and drove to the ground. It was a fairly small ground, two stands, one large bank of open terracing, and a tiny terrace behind the other goal. I didn't have a ticket for the game, but this was not a problem. The English fans were placed along the side of the pitch in two pens although there were also a few on the small bank of terracing behind the goal on our left. Those who had purchased tickets in advance from the England supporters club were put in one pen and the rest of the fans were allowed to pay at the turnstiles. The cost of a ticket at the turnstiles was considerably less than the FA had been charging in England. The FA always seemed quite happy to rip off the England fans at every given opportunity. They were assisted by the English police and the Government who often made outrageous statements and promises as to the dire consequences you faced if you so much as sneezed at the wrong person whilst travelling abroad. None of the threats of imprisonment, travelling embargoes, or indeed unavailability of tickets ever materialised, and once you had returned from a successful trip, you always felt like you had got one over on the UK authorities.

On the large open bank of terracing to our right, the main bulk of Poles stood. Most of them were skinheads and were dressed in green flight jackets. Suddenly, some of them turned their jackets inside out to reveal the bright orange lining. The two different gangs then proceeded to fight each other throughout the rest of the game. These skirmishes were certainly more interesting than the football and kept all of us amused on a bitterly cold night.

The game finished 1-1, a fine result which meant that England would be in Sweden for the finals the following year. Our pleasure at qualifying did not prevent us from ripping the plastic benches from the concrete terracing and throwing them at the police and journalists stood on the touchline directly in front of us. I think the true reason for this violent behaviour was to put us in the mood to fight the Poles, who no doubt would be waiting for us in large numbers outside the ground. We were kept in the ground for ages while the police concentrated on dispersing the Poles. The monotony was lifted by the sight of a couple of Chelsea fans driving a mini tractor onto the pitch. I don't know how they managed to steal the tractor or where from, but they continued driving until the stewards finally managed to grab them. I think they managed to run back to the terracing before they were arrested too.

Once we were let out of the ground, we were escorted back to the town. The police had successfully cleansed the streets of Polish skinheads and the long walk was surprisingly quiet. At one stage, we sent the police into a bit of a panic when we suddenly started running, then walking, then crossed over the road. They didn't know what to make of this strange behaviour and must have thought we were planning some kind of attack. In actual fact we were just playing up.

We returned to the hotel, which was kept under heavy police protection all night. The prostitutes were waiting for the return of the English and quite a few boys used their services. One group of lads decided to have a whip round to see if they could raise enough money to get one of the girls to allow them to piss all over her. One of the girls agreed to be pissed on, but when it came down to it, none of the lads had the nerve to go through with the act. One of the boys took the money and took the girl upstairs himself. The following morning he advised us that he had not worn a jacket and was now in great pain. He received no sympathy from any of us.

We made our way back to Berlin the following morning and had just enough time to have a good look around the city before catching our flight back to London. It certainly looked better in the day time. We also bumped into a couple of Chelsea fans who had been arrested in Berlin on the Tuesday night. They had only just been released from custody and were keen to hear what had happened in Poland. When we told them the story of the Chelsea fans hijacking the small tractor, they were gutted they had missed the game. They knew who the culprits were and couldn't wait to hear the full story.

Czechoslovakia, 1992

ENGLAND HAD QUALIFIED for the 1992 European Championships in Sweden, and in preparation for the tournament a couple of friendly internationals were arranged. One of the away games that caught my attention was the visit to Prague in March, 1992. Prague was supposed to be a beautiful city, the jewel in the crown of the Eastern block, and since the demise of communism, Westerners could travel there fairly easily.

The European Championships were only a couple of months away and I had been saving hard for the trip to Sweden. I had heard all the horror stories about the cost of living in Scandinavia and wanted to ensure I had enough money to enjoy the trip. Nonetheless, when I heard that our friend from Arsenal was arranging a two night break to Prague, I gladly handed my money over. Once again the cost of the trip only included flights and accommodation, but I was never bothered about travelling without match tickets and as this game was only a meaningless friendly, I didn't give the matter another thought.

I met up with the others in a pub in North London and after a couple of beers we ordered some cabs to take us to Heathrow. There were about 15 of us on the trip, the usual faces from Arsenal, Chelsea, Millwall and Boro. At the airport, we also met up with a lad from Cumbria who used to work at a nuclear plant. We christened him Ready-Brek in recognition of the red glow emanating from his body as a result of being subject to so much radiation.

We took our places on the aeroplane and were pleased to see our former England and brothel star in the seats next to us. The last time he had been spotted on an England trip was when he was sat in a den of vice in Poznan. 'All right mate, any good brothels in Prague?' we asked.

He seemed quite embarrassed at our line of questioning, and when he failed to give us any hints, we spent the rest of the journey verbally abusing him. It won't go down as one of his favourite trips, but in no time we had landed in Prague and taxis took us to our hotel in the heart of the city centre. A shower and a shave were the order of the day before meeting up in the hotel bar to sample the legendary

Czech beer. Our taste buds were in lager heaven as the most beautiful lager in the world was enthusiastically consumed. The lager tasted even nicer when we converted the local currency into sterling and discovered that a pint of lager was cheaper than a bar of chocolate back home. To be fair, the hotel bar was a little more expensive, about 80p a pint, but it still represented a bargain when compared to London prices

After a few hours sampling the various different lagers on sale in the hotel, we became restless and decided to go into the town to check out the night life. Our first port of call, was a bar called The Star Bar. It was brimming with gorgeous girls and I couldn't believe my luck when they made a point of coming over and chatting to us. Surrounded by beautiful girls and drinking the tastiest and cheapest lager I had ever come across, I couldn't have been happier. It soon dawned on me that the Star Bar was no ordinary pub though. The bar mats advertised the fact that the girls would do anything to keep the customers happy, and there were rooms available for hire upstairs, if you so desired.

We turned down their advances and continued on our bar crawl around Prague. It was dark by now, but from what I could see, Prague looked like any other Eastern European city. There were certainly plenty of bars around, but many of them were dingy looking basement bars. The natives were not particularly friendly, apart from the prostitutes in The Star Bar, and no one made any effort to speak to us. From what I could make out, German was the second language and very few people attempted to speak any English.

The general unfriendliness of the local people did not dampen our spirits though. How could you not enjoy yourself when the cost of a round of drinks for 15 people set you back only a couple of pounds? The alcohol was bound to take effect sooner rather than later, and after a few hours of solid drinking, the behaviour of our little mob started to worsen. We left the bar to try to find a night club. In one of the main streets, we came across a narrow doorway with a neon sign above the door informing us that there was a disco bar upstairs, but a huge Neanderthal bouncer blocked our entrance. A few of us were busy trying to persuade the bouncer to let us in when I heard the unmistakable sound of England fans, somewhere in the distance. There was no singing and chanting, just the noise of a roar followed by police sirens. It sounded like it was kicking off somewhere, but we were torn between going to the disco and trying to find out what was happening elsewhere.

Our dilemma was resolved when the mob of England fans appeared in our street. There was only a handful of them, but as they came towards us, we recognised them as some of Chelsea's boys. A couple of them had gone to Swansea with us, a year earlier. They were decent lads and could be relied upon in any dangerous situation. However, the difference between them and the majority of us was the fact that we were always just out to enjoy ourselves. If trouble found us, then we were well prepared for it and in many cases we relished the excitement and danger. However, we were just as happy to have a drink and a piss take. The Chelsea lads on the other hand travelled to matches with the sole intention of causing havoc wherever they went and fighting any foreigner they came across. They were nice guys, but they were fucking crazy!

They came over to see how we were and what we were up to. They had flown to Frankfurt and travelled on to Prague by rail. They were well pissed, but they were still clued up enough to realise that there had been some sort of an argument with the bouncer. 'Are these cunts not letting us in 'cos we're English?' asked one of the Chelsea boys.

It wasn't really the fact that we were English that was causing the problem. We were a large group of pissed up lads and not really the sort of people the bouncer wanted in his club. We could have been German, Dutch, or Japanese, but we were still not going to be allowed in. The Chelsea lads were in no mood to listen to reason though and one of them attacked the bouncer. Before the fight could develop into a full scale brawl, we noticed the police approaching. They had been following the Chelsea fans all night and so were not as stupid as they looked. The police mingled in with us and were trying to tell us something, but we couldn't comprehend what was being said. The Chelsea lads told us they were going off to some other pub where they had heard there might be some action. We made our excuses and walked off the other way. We ended up back in our hotel bar, where we continued drinking into the early hours, before crashing out in a drunken stupor.

Despite the amount of lager we had drunk the previous night, a few of us awoke early and decided to have a better look around the town. Once again, my first impressions of the city were not complimentary. The buildings were drab and quite depressing. However, we were obviously in the wrong part of town because after a while we found ourselves in the middle of a huge square, surrounded on all sides by incredible buildings. This is what most tourists visited Prague to see and we were quite pleased with ourselves that we had taken the opportunity to be normal tourists too for a change. A few photographs were taken before we reverted back to being typical English fans.

We had heard rumours that a McDonalds had recently opened in Prague, the first one in the whole of Czechoslovakia. We went off in search of the burger bar, and when we eventually found it I couldn't believe my eyes. There were hundreds of people queuing up and many were taking photographs of their entire family posing underneath the famous McDonalds sign. This strange behaviour really brought it home to me how difficult their lives must have been under communist rule. Things were changing for the better for these people and that could only be a good thing.

My appreciation of their harsh lives did not prevent us from being out of order. We pushed to the front of the queues and ordered our food. A few of us were not happy with the quality of our food and we complained to the staff. They didn't speak English and couldn't understand what our grievances were - after all, the Czech people appeared to be over the moon with their burgers. Some of us wanted our burgers without relish or gherkins, and although we had made this clear when ordering, the pre-packed burgers were still served with relish and gherkins.

The burgers were thrown onto the floor in anger while the locals looked on dumbstruck. Many of them had waited years to eat a hamburger and had saved for weeks to be able to afford a meal. When their moment of destiny had finally arrived, it was ruined by the anti-social behaviour of our group. To add insult to injury, we also started ripping up the Czech bank notes, which were virtually worthless to us anyway. Our behaviour certainly didn't endear us to the locals, but at the time we found it mildly amusing.

After our lunch, we returned to a bar in the city centre. One of the West Ham lads who was part of their arrogant mob in Sardinia turned up in the bar. He was on his own and came over to chat to us. He was trying to be friendly, but a few of us had a bit of the hump with him. When he was with his West Ham boys he wanted to take everyone on, particularly the Millwall boys, but now he was on his own, he suddenly wanted to be chums. It soon became clear he was not welcome, and rather wisely, he chose to leave the bar and went off to try to make friends elsewhere. I had no sympathy for him because you can't have it both ways at England games. Would he have been friendly if he was with 30 West Ham and one of us tried to join them? Judging by their behaviour at previous games, I very much doubt it. He was also lucky the crazy Chelsea fans were not with us.

Eventually it was time to make our way to the ground and again we hired a few cabs to take us across the city to the football stadium. It was a strange set up, with a couple of stadiums right next to each other on top of a steep hill on the edge of the city. None of us had tickets, but we were quickly advised that you could pay cash at the turnstile. The cost of admission was approximately 30 pence. I don't know how much the FA were selling tickets to England travel club members for back home, but you can bet your bottom dollar it was considerably more than 30 pence.

We waited outside the ground to see if any local hard nuts had come out for a dig at the infamous English football hooligans. A small mob of local skinheads strutted past staring at us in an effort to intimidate us, but their stares were met by loud laughter which had the desired effect of embarrassing the wannabee hooligans.

The main bulk of the England fans started arriving soon afterwards. They had flown to Prague, were put straight on to coaches, and then escorted directly to the ground by the police. Their trip had probably cost substantially more than ours, but they had not seen any of the city or had a good drink. I couldn't understand the mentality of someone who would travel to football in this way. It just appeared to me to be a waste of effort.

Just before kick-off we made our way into the ground. We stood for the national anthem and then headed for the bar. The cost of a pint in the bar underneath the stand was equivalent to just under 20 pence. As a result, we barely took any notice of the game. As we sat drinking, a few of the other England fans realised that you could walk right round the ground, go under the stands, and enter the home end. Behind one of the goals, the Czech skinheads were clearly visible. Like the Polish skinheads, they had turned their green flight jackets inside out and the bright orange lining was now clearly visible. I didn't understand the significance of this behaviour - perhaps it was some sort of macho mating routine East European skinheads indulge in when they are on the pull.

About ten Portsmouth and Chelsea lads were going around trying to get us to mob up and attack the skinheads in their own end. We were too busy drinking our beer to be bothered to get up and join in the fun and games, and in any case, we figured that these ten lads were more than capable of doing the skinheads without any assistance.

They set off for the other end and we settled down on the bench seats to watch developments unfold. Suddenly, the Czech skinheads raced to the back of the terrace. They obviously knew the English boys were below them and at first they looked quite game. Their bravery didn't last though. The English steamed onto the terrace, chasing the skinheads to the front. With nowhere else to run, the skinheads cowered in terror as the Portsmouth and Chelsea boys battered them into submission. The police swiftly moved in and baton charged the English out of the home end. They returned to our section very pleased with themselves. It had only been a brief skirmish, but they had proved a point to the skinheads and had kept us amused.

The game itself was very poor and ended up as a draw. We returned to the city centre to continue drinking the lager, and not surprisingly, the skinheads failed to make any effort to confront us. After a while we returned to the hotel and continued drinking into the early hours.

The following morning, we reluctantly set off for the airport. This time, Ludo, the Czechoslovakian goalkeeper who played for West Ham was on our flight. He also took plenty of stick, primarily from the Millwall lads, but credit where credit is due. Ludo took it all quite well. He smiled and laughed throughout the flight, even when he was bombarded with new potatoes.

The football had been very boring and only played a very small part in the trip. There had only been a couple of violent incidents, but most of our time was spent drinking and taking the piss out of everyone we met. All in all, it had been a fantastic trip to a wonderful city. It will always go down as one of my favourite away trips of that era. It just went to prove that you didn't need trouble to have a good time. The police, by and large, had left us to get on with it and apart from a couple of isolated incidents, we had behaved ourselves. It showed me what a good time could be had without the need to resort to violence. However, I didn't learn my lesson for another year.

Sweden, 1992

ENGLAND HAD BEEN drawn against Yugoslavia and France in the qualifying stages of the European championships. Both games were to be played in Malmo, in the south of Sweden, just a short ferry ride from Copenhagen.

I was certain England would qualify from the group, so I decided to miss our opening game against Yugoslavia in the hope that we would travel on to Gothenburg or Stockholm for the later stages of the tournament. Three of us booked up for the trip and decided to fly to Copenhagen two days before the France game, thus enabling us to enjoy a night out in both Copenhagen and Malmo before watching the game against France.

Our plans took a set back when it was announced that Yugoslavia would not participate in the tournament as a result of the conflict in the Balkans. At the last minute, they were replaced by Denmark. I was gutted at missing this game as I knew thousands of Danish fans would make the short journey across to Malmo, ensuring a full house and a lively atmosphere.

In the end, I watched the game in a pub in England. There were no reports of any trouble and by all accounts there was quite a party atmosphere. The Swedish authorities had set up beer tents where the alcohol was considerably cheaper than in the normal bars. This sounded like a great idea, as the cost of drink over there was nearly enough to prevent me from making the trip in the first place.

We flew over to Copenhagen the day after the game against Denmark on a British Airways flight that left London at tea time. We had spent all lunch time in the pub and on top of this there were complimentary drinks being served throughout the flight. By the time we landed at Copenhagen, we were well and truly pissed. We managed to catch a bus into the city centre and were dropped off close to the train station. There were quite a few English guys loitering about and they advised us to visit the tourist information office who would be able to fix us up with some accommodation for the night.

We made our way to the tourist information office where a stunning Danish girl was waiting to help us. She warned us that the price of accommodation was extremely high in the city and there was very little availability. We asked her for details of the cheapest hotel room she had available. She eventually found a hotel that was prepared to accommodate all of us in one room for a fairly reasonable price, but felt that she had to warn us that it was in the heart of the red light district. This did not deter us in the slightest. Booking arrangements were made and we quickly headed off to find our digs.

The taste for beer was still with us so we dumped our luggage and headed off into the town. It was a beautiful summer's evening and Copenhagen certainly was one of the most picturesque cities I had ever been to. The glorious views were made even better by the fact that everywhere you looked you couldn't fail to see stunning girls. Even stranger was the fact that all of them were friendly and always smiling. It was certainly not what I was used to with the girls back home. In London, even the ugly ones were often aloof and moody.

We went from bar to bar, drinking more Elephant lager, chatting to the local girls, and meeting up with other English fans. It didn't seem to get any darker as the night wore on, which was a strange feeling as it still felt like it was six o'clock in the evening when in fact it was rapidly approaching midnight. It was a shame we were so pissed. We could barely stand, let alone get our words out, but had we been less drunk, I'd like to think we would have pulled some girls.

We ended up in a cafe bar, sniffing amyl-nitrate, drinking more lager, and slobbering over the local girls. It was about five o'clock in the morning, but it had hardly turned dark all night. We decided enough was enough, and returned to our digs for some much needed rest. We woke up again a few hours later, packed our bags, and made our way to the train station. A few other England fans were there and they provided us with a ferry timetable for the trip to Malmo. One of us had a gas canister hidden in his pants, but the other lads told us that a few boys had been stopped at Malmo and been refused entry into the country when they had been caught smuggling CS gas. Rather than get rid of it completely though, the lad decided to hide it in his bag.

We caught the ferry over to Malmo and got chatting to a couple of Swedish girls who were just as attractive and friendly as the Danish girls. They told us that alcohol was looked down upon in Sweden and was ridiculously expensive. The major brands were brewed under licence in Sweden and it was against the law to sell strong lager. As a result of this, many of the girls from Malmo regularly crossed over to Copenhagen for a good night out. When we arrived in Malmo, we were stopped by customs officers and searched. Our bags were opened and the contents examined. The canister was spotted and the smuggler taken away for questioning. The canister was confiscated, but fortunately the smuggler was allowed into the country after his personal details were taken down and he was given an on the spot fine of £120. Fortunately, he was allowed to pay the fine when he returned to England, although I very much doubt that he ever did cough up the money.

Other England fans were not so fortunate. We had arranged to meet two of our friends in Malmo, but when we turned up at their hotel the other lads in their party told us that the Swedish customs officers had refused to let them into the country on the advice of English football intelligence officers. They were put on the first plane back to London. A couple of other lads had been arrested after a drunken brawl in the street with a couple of local lads. They were now incarcerated in the local nick. Their misfortune meant that there was a spare room in the hotel, so it saved us the bother of walking round Malmo all afternoon searching for accommodation. Every cloud has a silver lining.

After a brief kip and a shower we took to the streets again to have a look around Malmo. Like Copenhagen, the town was clean, pretty, and appeared to be populated entirely by gorgeous females. In the middle of the town square was a large beer tent. The majority of English fans were drinking in and around the tent and generally befriending the local girls. Only a handful of police kept a discreet eye on the fans. The atmosphere was very laid back, nothing like the hostile atmosphere experienced in Italy two years earlier. There were also plenty of food stalls, selling relatively cheap snacks. All of these stalls were operated by Turks or Lebanese.

We left the majority of the England fans drinking in the beer tent and went in search of some local bars, There were plenty around and most of them were done out very nicely. Nearly every bar we visited had a roulette table and a gorgeous blonde girl serving behind the bar. I was starting to believe I had truly discovered paradise.

We spent the next few hours drinking, chatting and gambling. Unfortunately, none of us seemed to be getting drunk and although we were spending plenty of money we were not getting the desired effect. A quick check of the alcoholic percentage levels on the bottles explained why so we decided to return to the beer tent to see if anything was happening.

It was now fairly late and most of the England fans had been drinking all day. The town square was packed with England fans and local girls. Everyone appeared to be drunk, but in party spirits and the police and a number of guardian angel steward types were maintaining a discreet eye on proceedings. Suddenly, a loud cheer went up from the crowd. A drunken English fan had made it onto the roof of the tent and was now dancing away, generally making a fool of himself in front of the crowd. Everyone laughed along with the idiot and after a few minutes he decided to make his way back to the ground.

Every time he nearly reached ground level, the police were waiting to arrest him. It became a game of chase as the police tried to predict where he was going to get down. Eventually, the lad gave up, returned to the square and was promptly arrested. It was a bit harsh, but only to be expected really. As he was led away, other English lads picked up chairs and tables and steamed into the handful of police now present in the square. The ferocity of the attack obviously shocked the police and they scattered. The guardian angels tried to intervene, but they were also attacked. One of them had his prized beret pinched from his head. It also scared the local girls who started screaming and running away.

Within a matter of seconds, the carnival atmosphere had changed to one more normally associated with England fans. The police were chased out of the square and those that were caught took severe beatings. Car windows were smashed and shop windows were looted. The food stalls were knocked over and the Turks and Lebanese attacked. In the end, there was no one left to fight with so the English fans literally smashed everything they could get their hands on. I was stunned by the speed of the change in atmosphere.

Police sirens grew louder and louder as the riot police converged on the war zone. A group of riot police were spotted in a side street. Hundreds of fans charged down the side street causing the riot police to panic. They turned and ran for their lives. One of the officers was caught, dragged to the ground and kicked unconscious. This took place right next to a canal and a number of the fans tried to pick him up and throw him in the murky water. They were prevented from doing so only by the return of more riot police who came to their colleague's rescue just in time to save his life.

The English fans were chased down this street, parallel to the canal and past a hotel where a bride and groom were just setting off on their honeymoon. Their romantic moment was ruined by the sight of hundreds of English fans running past them, closely followed by the Swedish riot squad. Sardinia all over again.

The sight of one of their colleague's nearly getting killed had angered the riot police who were determined to seek revenge. Back in the square, the police came under a hail of missiles, but the riot police were more than a match for this and easily forced the England fans to disperse. The running battles continued, but the police seemed determined to clear the streets completely of any English fans.

We had seen enough and decided to return to one of the bars we had been drinking in earlier on in the evening. The mood in the bar was very calm, and the people who had remained in the bar genuinely weren't aware of the carnage that was taking place in the streets outside. After a while, a few more England fans came into the bar. They were now saying the streets were very dangerous. The police were detaining any England fans they apprehended, and there were also now gangs of irate Turks and Lebanese looking for revenge for the fact that a lot of their stalls had been attacked and robbed. It certainly sounded like a dodgy situation and was so much different to the atmosphere in the town just an hour earlier.

We sat in the bar until closing time when we were asked to leave. Reluctantly we left, but fortunately there was a tram stop only a short distance from the bar and we carefully made our way to the stop, keeping an eye out for angry Turks at all times. Fortunately, a tram arrived without much delay, but when it pulled up, you couldn't help but notice that a number of windows had been shattered. When the doors opened, a few English guys were on the tram rubbing their eyes and nursing their bruises. They told us that the tram had pulled up at the stop before our one, and a gang of Turks attacked it armed with baseball bats and gas. The Turks had left the area immediately after the attack and were last seen heading towards where we had just come from. A lucky escape indeed for us. We got off the tram at the stop nearest our hotel and walked the short distance to the hotel without any further problems.

When we returned to the square the following morning, the pretty girls had been replaced by scores of angry looking riot police.

The party atmosphere had vanished, and for the first time on the trip, I felt unwelcome. It was a crying shame because it would have been great to have had a nice week in Sweden, but as a result of our behaviour the previous night, we could now only expect the usual kind of barbaric treatment reserved for England fans by police forces throughout Europe.

To be fair, the Swedish authorities had made an effort to help us enjoy ourselves. The police presence had been kept to a minimum and entertainment had been provided. Unfortunately, the behaviour of a large minority of fans meant that the party was now well and truly over.

We were playing France later that afternoon and the handful of French fans in the town looked absolutely terrified every time they came across a group of England fans. We wandered off to the ground in search of match tickets, and as usual they were fairly easy to come by. When the match kicked off, even the atmosphere in the ground seemed a little muted, although this may have had something to do with the awful game. It ended up 0-0 and was only memorable for a Basil Boli head butt on Stuart Pearce.

We made our way back to our favourite bar in the town centre. By now, I was a little pissed off and decided that in the morning I would return to Copenhagen and spend the rest of the week drinking quality lager, watching the football on TV, and trying to pull some of the beautiful Danish girls. As this was to be our last night in Sweden, we decided to get as pissed as possible. We ended up drinking the bottles of Bacardi we had purchased at the duty free shop at the airport, and the rest of the night is a complete blur, but the following day was spent nursing the worst hangover I have ever experienced.

I woke up late in the afternoon and discovered I was on my own in the hotel room. I suspected that the rest of the lads had gone back to the pub in the town and I reluctantly made my way to join them. There were very few English fans left in Malmo and the streets were virtually deserted as I walked through the square. The pub, however, was packed. The rest of the lads had livened up considerably more than I had, and were now eagerly discussing plans for the trip to Stockholm. England were to play the host nation in the capital city and the thought of taking on the infamous Black Army was a mouth watering prospect.

The Black Army were supposedly a fearless gang of hooligans who had been planning to attack England fans en masse in Stockholm. These stories were widely reported in the papers prior to our departure, but differed wildly to the experience of most English fans who had been to Stockholm in 1989.

Any ideas I had of spending the next few days in Copenhagen were quickly forgotten as everyone decided that we had to defend the honour of England against the Stockholm street gangs. We headed up to the train station and booked the tickets on the overnight train to Stockholm. I returned to the bar and spent the rest of the afternoon sleeping off the previous night's indulgences. When the other lads woke me to say it was time to catch the train, I rubbed my eyes and followed the rest of the lads to the station.

The station was packed with Swedish police and undercover English police. The word on the streets was that the English police were identifying known hooligans and advising the Swedish police to refuse to let them on the Stockholm bound train. The Swedish police were also trying to recognise faces from the disorder that took place in the town square two nights earlier. All this security added to the growing tensions in Malmo and I for one was relieved when we all boarded the train without any problems and left Malmo for Stockholm.

My hangover at long last started to disappear and I enjoyed the over night journey, wasting away the hours failing miserably to pull some East German girls. They must have been lesbians.

The train eventually pulled into Stockholm central station in the middle of the morning rush hour. We were met by a welcoming committee of police who were recording us on video as we left the train to begin our latest search for cheap accommodation. Our dishevelled appearance clearly marked us out as strangers in yet another city packed with beautiful females. The tourist information office managed to fix us up with some digs in one of the seedier parts of town and so we trampled through the streets of Stockholm with our bags over our shoulders, drooling over every girl we passed.

We didn't hang around in the hotel and after a wash and a change of clothes, we went for a look around the city. It truly was yet another beautiful city and I was amazed at the cleanliness of the streets. The price of food and alcohol was quite steep, but certainly not as bad as we had been led to believe.

The main bulk of the England fans were congregating in the bars in and around the central station. There was a very relaxed atmosphere and the hostility that had marred the last couple of days in Malmo had disappeared, for the time being anyway. The police kept a discreet eye on the fans, but as far as I know, there were no violent incidents all afternoon.

As the night wore on and we slowly started getting more and more drunk, the number of girls hitting the bars and clubs increased dramatically. Nearly every girl you approached was stunning and also friendly. It seemed they had all come out to meet the English hooligans. Many of them also spoke better English than a lot of us so language certainly wasn't a barrier here.

Our table of eight or nine lads was approached by a large Swedish woman in her late thirties. She was a little past her sell by date, but was friendly and definitely up for the cup. She was trying to get us all to return to her flat. We warned her of the consequences she would have to face if we all went back. She would certainly be a busy hostess and would definitely have trouble walking in the morning. All this just seemed to excite her even more. Her hopes were dashed a little when two other younger girls joined us. Both girls were stunning and were not shy in making their intentions clear. It turned out that one of the girls lived with the other girl's brother. Despite this strange set up, they were both clearly out on the pull and agreed to come with us when we decided to find another bar. The older woman wasn't invited.

I had been chatting to one of these girls and was quietly confident that I would be going back to her place later on to sample some proper Swedish hospitality. Before finding the other bar, a few of us fancied a bite to eat and were sitting in a burger bar with the two girls when a mob of English fans came running past. Believing that there was some sort of trouble happening out on the streets, I left the girls to it and decided to take a look outside. Nothing much was happening so I returned to the girl to carry on flirting.

Unfortunately for me, my mate, Andy, had used my 30 second absence to move in on my girl and was clearly dazzling her with some of his favourite lines. I wasn't bitter though and left him to try to shag the ugly blonde bimbo while I went off to the bar with the other English lads who had failed to pull.

Me and the other ugly England fans spent the rest of the night drinking in pleasant and friendly bars in the centre of Stockholm. At the end of the night we returned to our hotel, still in good spirits despite our appalling strike rate with the local beauties. We consoled ourselves with the argument that we were on international duty and should be leaving the girls alone. It didn't heal our wounds.

An hour or so later one of the lads returned to our room with one of the girls. At first, we pretended to be asleep, but our childish giggles alerted the two lovers. Andy was staying in another room, but had still not returned from his night out with my chick so we told the passionate couple to bugger off to the empty room if they wanted to shag each other.

Before they left, the pair of them sat down on the bed and had a quick chat with us. The girl had taken her shoes off and when they left to go into the other room, she left her shoes behind. One of the other lads who was staying in our room had also pulled a local girl and had wandered off with her at the end of the night. Earlier on in the trip, he had made the mistake of telling us that his mum had packed his bag for him. No doubt, she would also empty the bag on his return and so we decided to hide the girl's shoes in his bag. This would leave him with some explaining to do when he got home.

A couple of hours later the girl from next door quietly entered our room. We were still wide awake, but pretended that she had just woken us. 'Have you seen my shoes?' she asked. 'I think I left them in here earlier.'

We carried out an extensive search of the room, but surprise, surprise, none of us could find her shoes. 'I can't go home without my shoes. How will I explain that to my boyfriend?'

'I'm sure you'll think of something. Tell him you got caught up in the middle of some Scousers raring up at everyone and they nicked your shoes.'

She was a very worried girl as she left our hotel. The prospect of returning home to her boyfriend in the early hours of the morning with no shoes was not a pleasant thought for this shy, retiring Stockholm beauty. Still, it made us chuckle.

Shortly after she left our room, another one of our room mates returned. He was clearly making an effort to be quiet so we decided to pretend we were fast asleep. Taking great care, he quietly shut the door, stripped down to his boxer shorts and got into bed. He had a huge smile beaming all over his smug face and was clearly very pleased with his sexual exploits. As we kept an eye on him, he let out a quiet cry of 'Yessss!' before turning over to try to go to sleep. His behaviour was enough for us all to burst out laughing, causing him to turn red as he suddenly realised we had been watching him ever since he had opened the door.

When the laughter eventually died down, we started to quiz him about the girl we had seen him with earlier on in the night. 'Did you do her?'

'Yeah, she was brilliant, much better than any English sort.'

'Where did you go?'

'Back to her gaff'

'A flat or a house? Who else lived there? How did you get there? How did you get back?'

Our questions were coming thick and fast and it was clear that his story was not water tight. Eventually, he admitted that they had only gone for a walk in a park.

'But, you've been gone ages, what have you been doing all this time?'

'Talking. She's a lovely girl. I gave her my telephone number and she's going to come to England soon.'

'Forget all that bollocks, did you shag her, yes or no?'

'Sort of.'

'What do you mean by that?'

'I got a blow job'.

He was embarrassed, but clearly very pleased with himself. He had got further than any of us sad losers, but in reality that wasn't too hard. Still, he had spent all night buying this girl drinks in the bars, had spent a few hours alone with her after the bars had shut, and at the end of the day all he had to show for it was a blow job. To be fair to him, she did turn up in England a couple of months later and she was certainly a good looking girl.

We nodded off to sleep, but only a few hours later, Andy burst into our room to tell me in person all about the girl he stole from me. To rub salt into my wounds, he meticulously recalled every detail of his night of passion, but basically he had gone back to her flat and given her his two inches of England. His story was water tight and despite my best efforts, I could find no cracks. Lucky bugger!

When we got up, we had breakfast, washed ourselves, and walked into the centre of Stockholm. England were playing the host nation today, and for the first time Stockholm was alive with Swedish fans. They were nearly all dressed in yellow and blue outfits and certainly did not appear to offer any kind of a threat to the England fans. Most of the England fans were still drinking in the bars near the central station, but we had heard a rumour that there was a Stone Island shop somewhere in the town so we decided to try to find it to see if we could pick up any bargains.

The shop was a good ten minute walk from the station, and when we found it, there were quite a few other English lads milling around outside. They told us that there wasn't much stock left, but the prices were reasonable and the shoplifting was easy. Most of the shelves were bare though, and of the garments that remained, most had the distinctive Stone Island label missing from the left arm sleeve.

We bought a couple of sweatshirts, took these back to the hotel, and then returned to the bars near the station. A few of us still didn't have tickets for the game and in view of the fact that we were playing the host nation and the game was a sell out, we knew it would be difficult securing any. There were very few ticket touts in the city centre, but we expected to see more nearer the ground. However, I had met a lad in Malmo who was a member of the England supporters club. He had a ticket for the Sweden game which he needed to pick up from the supporters club temporary office outside the ground before the game, but as luck would have it, he had run out of money in Malmo and had had to return home to England. He told me that if I turned up at the office claiming to be him, there was a chance they might hand the ticket over to me. I suspected that I would need some sort of identification to prove that I was claiming to be, but I thought I would give it a go and memorised his name and address. His name was Steve Pratt and he came from Brentwood.

A couple of hours to go before kick-off and we decided to leave the city centre and make our way to the ground on the underground. Although the city was buzzing with excited Swedes, nothing much was happening and there was certainly very little hope of finding a spare ticket. The underground stations in Stockholm were very different to the polluted and dangerous ones found all over London. As you walked down the escalators , it was like walking into a natural cave and was a very eerie feeling. The walls had not been plastered, they had just been left as they were.

There were only a few England fans on the tube, but when we arrived at the stadium, a few more were milling around. There were no touts so I wandered off to find the supporters club office. There was a small queue, but after a small delay I found myself at the desk where a young English girl was waiting to help me. 'I've reserved a ticket, but lost my membership card.'

'Fine, can you give me your name, address, date of birth, and membership number.'

I expected some questions, but even so, I felt myself going red as I struggled to remember my personal details. 'I'm Steve Pratt from, er, Brentford', I replied, deliberately omitting to give her the rest of the information which I obviously didn't know.

'Brentford or Brentwood?'

I had forgotten. I guessed the piece of paper in front of her contained the magic words needed to releae my ticket and tried to sneak a look. I couldn't see the address though and so decided to take a gamble.

'Brentwood,' I replied.

The look on her face made it clear that she didn't believe I was Mr Pratt, although I certainly felt like one. 'Mr Pratt, what is your full home address?'

The question was asked in a rather triumphant tone of voice. She knew she had me beaten, but I wouldn't back down. I pretended to ignore her, looking out of the window as if I had just spotted someone I knew and casually waited for her to hand over my match ticket. She repeated the question and I apologised for being so distant.

'Excuse me, I've just seen my mate, I'll be back in a minute.'

I turned and left the building and didn't turn round until I was well clear. When I returned to my mates, I discovered that the only other lad not to have a ticket had just bought one off another England fan. This meant that Mr Pratt was the only person without a ticket.

The area outside the ground was full of high rise blocks of flats and I didn't fancy being left on my own outside the ground during the game. I left the others to it and went off on my own in search of the elusive ticket. I asked at the ticket office if there were any spare tickets, but unsurprisingly the reply was negative.

With about 20 minutes to go to kick-off, I struck lucky. A young Swedish fan had a spare ticket which he was willing to sell for face value. I quickly completed the deal, well aware that I would be sat with the Swedish fans and not in the England end with my fellow countrymen. This didn't concern me too much though. It was hardly Poland away, and from what I had seen most of the Swedish fans were polite and friendly.

I queued up for entrance to the home end, surrounded by boisterous Swedish fans. They didn't look too menacing, but the sheer volume of fans was quite intimidating. As I reached the turnstile, a security guard said something to me in Swedish. I tried to ignore him, but he was not to be fooled. He called the police over, and my heart pounded furiously as they spoke to each other. Surely, I wasn't going to get arrested after trying so hard to obtain a ticket? The policeman came over to me and said in clear English, 'You are an English fan. You cannot come in here.'

The large gates into the ground were opened and I was escorted to the ticket office under the stand, where a few other English fans were being held by the police. After a short delay, we were asked to hand over our tickets to the police. As we did so, a pretty girl from the ticket office came over and handed us some other tickets. She explained that we were welcome in the ground, so long as we sat in the England end. This was fine by me and I left the ticket office overjoyed with my good fortune.

I tried to look for my mates but as kick-off time was only a couple of minutes away, I figured they would already be in the ground. I walked round to the England end and witnessed a few scuffles taking place between rival fans. The police were on top of the situation though so I decided to find my seat in the stand.

The bulk of the England fans were behind one of the goals, but the instructions on my ticket led me to the stand alongside the pitch which seemed to be reserved for the home fans. Fortunately, I was in the block right next to the official away end and there were plenty of other England fans in the seats with me.

I stood for the national anthem, took my seat and then jumped for joy again as England took the lead in the second minute of the match. Someone threw a bottle of water all over me, but I didn't care. I was in the ground, England were winning, and everything was looking fine and dandy. Until that is Thomas Brolin started dictating the game and inspired Sweden to take the lead. Our fading hopes of winning the game were dealt a severe blow when England supremo, Graham Taylor, took off England captain and legendary goal scorer, Gary Lineker and replaced him with Alan Smith. It was an incredible tactical blunder, and one I am sure Taylor will regret for the rest of his life. England went on to lose the game and so were out of the tournament. Taylor was relentlessly criticised by the media and labelled a turnip. The name was to stick, and to this day poor old Graham Taylor is universally known as Turniphead.

The Swedish nation partied like it was 1999. Fireworks exploded and lit up the night sky. The Swedes felt sure they were on their way to winning the tournament, and despite my obvious hurt at losing, I genuinely wished the Swedes the best of luck.

I left the ground and walked out into the street behind the England end. The police refused to let us go to the underground station until the rest of the England fans left the ground. We were kept waiting a few minutes until the rest of the fans were allowed to leave, but once outside, a number of England fans easily broke out of the police escort and headed away from the underground station. I mingled in with these lads who were clearly looking for some action. They were talking about walking back to Stockholm, but fortunately some of them realised how far it was and decided against it. We headed into the housing estate behind the stadium, but the police were following us at all times. The police presence was getting larger and larger and eventually we were forced to toe the line and were taken to the underground station.

The police escorted us on to a train which was heading to the central station where we felt the majority of England fans would be firming up. A few of us decided to stay on the tube at central station and get off at the next stop. This was close to the Stone Island shop. If the bulk of the English were fighting outside the main station, we reasoned this would provide the ideal opportunity for looting the Stone Island shop. All the police would be concentrating on the rival fans fighting while we would be getting away with hundreds of pounds worth of Stone Island gear. The idea soon spread like wildfire around the carriages and when the train pulled into the main station no one made an effort to disembark from the train. This mystified the police, but there was nothing they could do. At the next stop, hundreds of us alighted and made our way to street level to locate the shop. There were so many of us now, that it was highly unlikely that I would be able to get any goods in any case. This was a job for five or six lads, not two hundred or so.

Before we could find the Stone Island shop, a few of the lads discovered that there was a large square nearby. It had fountains in the middle and was packed with celebrating Swedish fans. The mob moved as one, approaching the square in silence as our planss for plundering were put to one side. When we reached the square, we charged at the Swedish fans, picking up bicycles and throwing them at the Swedes who quickly scattered. A gas canister was discharged by one of the English lads, but for some reason it landed in the middle of us, causing us to cough and splutter all over the square. Within seconds, the riot police converged on the square and baton charged us out of it and further away from the central station.

Each time, the police charge came to an end, the English mob regrouped, picked up bottles and other weapons, and ran back at them. The police responded by baton charging us further and further away from central station. As I was running through the streets of Stockholm, dodging blows to my head, I noticed that all the bars were packed with gorgeous girls staring at us with bemused expressions on their faces. I suddenly realised I no longer wanted to be part of this scene.

Once again, the police baton charge came to an end and the English fans regrouped and prepared for another attack on the police. It was clear that most of them were enjoying their escapades, but I had grown rather bored and just wanted to get out of the area. The constant running back and forth had become rather tedious and the thought of relaxing in a bar with a beer, surrounded by Swedish girls, was much more appealing. I disappeared down a narrow side street and left the police and the other fans to continue their fun and games. Although I knew the general direction of where I wanted to go, I was still worried about getting lost. I spotted a pretty girl walking towards me and decided to ask her for directions.

'Excuse me, do you know the way to the central station?' I asked.

She told me she wasn't sure as she was from Helsinki and didn't really know Stockholm that well. As she spoke, I realised how beautiful she was and very nearly fell in love with her there and then. As my mind wandered off to other parts of her body, I noticed a gang of Turks loitering around in the street.

I kept one eye on the Turks while the girl was chatting about English people in general and English fans in particular. I noticed the Turks walking towards us and quietly pointed out to the girl that if these Turks realised I was English, they would probably attack me. She also sensed the danger and started talking to me in her native language. She went one better, took my hand, and casually led me past the Turks and on to safety. I was incredibly relieved, said thank you to my heroine, and strolled off back towards the station. After a minute or so, I kicked myself so hard I nearly screamed.

What was I doing leaving this beauty on her own? I'm sure she would have gone for a drink with me, which might have led on to something beyond my wildest imagination. I turned around, but she had disappeared and I didn't fancy going back to find her in case the Turkish gang were still searching for dumb love-struck English fans.

I walked back towards the city centre, kicking drink cans in the street and cursing my own stupidity. How could I have been so stupid as to let this girl walk out of my life. Eventually, I realised where I was and decided to avoid the station and return to my hotel.

I met up with the other lads and we all discussed the game in depth. With England now out of the tournament, it was time for us to start making our journey home. However, our return flight ticket from Copenhagen was not valid for another three days. We certainly didn't have enough money to keep us going for three more days and pay the train fare back to Copenhagen. We had only bought a single train ticket to Stockholm in case we went on to Gothenburg for the next round or found ourselves being deported.

The following morning, we didn't shave, put on our dirty clothes, and walked down to the British Airways office in the town. We spun a lie about getting mugged and losing all our money. The girl fell for our cunning scheme and agreed to change our flight tickets to one leaving Stockholm later on that day.

We rushed back to our hotel, washed and shaved, and jumped on a bus to the airport. On arrival at Heathrow, the police rounded up the England fans from the plane, confiscated our passports, and led us away from passport control into a small office. We sat down as the police took our passports and went into a separate room. Every few minutes, a policeman would re-enter the office, clutching a passport. He called out the name of the passport holder, handed the passport back to the fan and asked which team he followed. Eventually, all the other fans had received back their passports and had left the office. I was left on my own for a few more minutes agonising as to why I was the only one remaining. At last, an officer approached clutching my passport. 'Alright, Colin,' he said as he handed my passport back to me. 'You're a Millwall supporter, aren't you?'

It wasn't a question really. He was deliberately making it clear that he knew I supported the Lions. The rest of the England fans had been asked who their teams were, but I hadn't. This concerned me deeply. How did he know who I was and how did he know I supported Millwall? I was friendly with quite a few lads who the police were obviously concerned about, and I suppose I was guilty by association. This was a frightening development because generally speaking, I was a law abiding citizen with a respectable job. I didn't like the idea of being on police files somewhere, but I still loved the excitement and fear that went hand in hand with travelling abroad as an England fan. And for the time being at least, I was not going to give up my hobby because of some cocky copper who was trying to make a point.

Spain, 1992

IN SEPTEMBER, 1992, England played a friendly against Spain in their first away game since the European Championships. Despite my concerns over the behaviour of the police at Heathrow, I still fancied making the trip. A week on the Costa Brava with my mates sounded a great idea.

When full details of the fixture were announced, I learned that the game was to be played in Santander, a bustling port on the north coast of Spain. This is a little off the beaten track as far as most English tourists are concerned, but I suspected that this was a deliberate ploy by the authorities to avoid the possibility of thousands of drunken English yobs rampaging through Llorett De Mar or Benidorm. A quick flick through the holiday brochures indicated that it was a 36 hour boat trip from England to Santander, or alternatively, you could take a short flight to Bilbao, a city that was just a short bus or train journey from Santander.

A few of us decided to make the trip and opted for the flight to Bilbao on the Tuesday before the game. We would spend Tuesday in Bilbao and then go to Santander early on the Wednesday morning. All day would be spent at leisure in Santander and we would obviously watch the game in the evening. We would return to Bilbao on the Thursday morning to catch our flight back to Blighty later that afternoon.

I arranged to meet my mate Andy, a butcher, in our local pub on the Tuesday morning. He was working in the morning and told me he would come straight from work, after showering and changing his clothes there. He turned up in the pub with another lad who he had been working with. His name was Nick and he was from Southend. He didn't have a flight ticket or a passport, but did not envisage any problems making it to Spain. This struck me as a bit odd, but he assured me he had often turned up at airports, demanding a seat on a flight despite not having a ticket or a passport. If he played up and threatened to phone *The Sun*, they usually gave in.

After a few beers, we caught a taxi over to Heathrow airport and tried to check in. 'Tickets and passports?' asked the check-in girl.

Nick started telling her his well worn hard luck story about how he had misplaced his ticket and passport. The girl listened attentively, but at the end of his speech she told him quite firmly that he would be travelling nowhere without a passport.

I expected him to go crazy and threaten to call his friends in Fleet Street, but he just accepted what she said without causing a scene. He made his excuses to us and returned to Southend. I couldn't understand the reasoning behind his strange behaviour. Maybe he just wanted to pretend that he really was going away and the only reason he didn't go was because he was prevented from doing so. Maybe he genuinely thought they'd let him travel.

We continued with the check-in procedure. As Andy had come straight from work, his bag contained a number of knives. He warned the check-in girl about the contents of his bag. She wouldn't let him take the knives on the flight for obvious reasons, but told us that they could to be taken with the rest of the luggage.

After checking in, we went to the bar for a drink where we bumped into a couple of friends from Boro we knew from previous trips. We had a drink together and joined the flight. On arrival at Bilbao airport, we passed through passport control without any problems, but had to go to the luggage carousel to pick up the knives. The rest of our bags had been taken on the flight as hand luggage. We waited next to the carousel with all the other passengers who were mainly Spanish. The police were keeping a fairly close eye on us, but when Andy picked up his set of butcher's knives from the luggage carousel, their behaviour towards us changed dramatically. We were questioned by the police and customs officers who could barely speak a word of English, but fortunately Andy managed to persuade them that the knives were merely a tool of his trade and not weapons for attacking Spanish football fans.

Once safely through passport control, we found a couple of taxis and asked the driver to take us into Bilbao, a rough and ready industrial port and one that was heavily polluted at that. I had heard numerous stories about Bilbao from English fans who went to the World Cup in Spain in 1982. The English had been based there in the qualifying stages of the tournament before moving on to Madrid for the second round.

The people of Bilbao are Basque and do not consider themselves Spanish, and generally speaking, they are a lot friendlier to the English than people from other parts of Spain. They do not fly the Spanish flag and often speak in their own dialect. There is also a terrorist organisation known as ETA who operate out of the Basque region of Spain and their primary aim is for the Basque region to become independent from Spain. Everywhere you went in Bilbao, there was political graffiti on the walls.

We were dropped off next to the river in the heart of the city. The river was filthy and stunk of sewerage and the streets were dark and menacing. Fortunately, there was a hotel close by and as luck would have it, there were vacancies available. The idea of walking round Bilbao with our bags in search of a hotel didn't really appeal and so we booked into the hotel, despite the seedy surroundings.

We didn't hang around the hotel and after the obligatory wash and change of clothes, we took to the streets in search of alcohol. Our trip took us into the old town, an area of narrow lanes and alleyways, packed with small bars, restaurants and tapas bars. Although the bars looked tiny from outside, once you entered, they were all long and narrow. They were also all packed with locals who weren't at all bothered by the appearance of four young English lads.

Each time we ordered a round of drinks, we were handed a receipt and advised to pay before we left. As the bars were all so busy, the bar staff did not notice that we would leave the bar without paying. It was so easy, and you could see why this would never catch on in England. Pubs would go out of business within a week.

We spent the next few hours crawling round every bar in the old town without paying for a single drink all evening. After a while, we decided to stay in one particular bar even though the chances were we would have to pay the bar bill at the end of the night. We sat in this bar drinking and chatting and generally just enjoying ourselves.

It was my shout and so I ordered another round of drinks. By now I was drinking vodka and orange, and when the barman went to serve my drink, he noticed he had run out of orange juice. He went into a back room to find some more, leaving a full bottle of vodka on the bar in front of us. Needless to say, we helped ourselves, quickly downing the whole bottle between us, without any mixers. When the barman returned and the bottle of vodka was nowhere to be seen, we convinced him that he had not left the bottle on the bar. He didn't fancy arguing and simply opened up a new bottle.

He must have become a little suspicious though, when in the space of a matter of minutes, the four of us turned from being a little merry to being absolutely wasted. The rest of the night is a complete blur, although some very strange photographs were taken.

When I awoke in the morning, my stomach felt like it was on fire as the vodka continued to pound away at my delicate stomach lining. The other lads were also suffering, but we managed to check out of the hotel by ten o'clock as we had been requested to do. We then went off into the town in search of the train station, but when we found it we were told that the quickest way to get to Santander was by bus. The next bus was leaving in one hour which left us enough time to hire a cab to take us on a whirlwind sight-seeing trip of Bilbao. In all honesty, there wasn't much to see. However, one place of interest for four football fans was the San Memes stadium, home of Athletic Bilbao. This was the scene of England's triumph over the French in the 1982 World Cup in the game in which Bryan Robson scored the fastest goal in the history of the tournament.

We made it back to the bus station in time for the departure to Santander. The journey took about an hour, and once we had left the city we travelled through some glorious scenery. The deep blue sea was on our right and rolling green hills to our left. As the others marvelled at the beauty of the landscape, I was doing my very best to avoid throwing up all over the Spanish girl sat next to me. She was obviously aware of my impending bout of sickness and started to look as worried as me. Fortunately for her, and the rest of the passengers, I managed to retain the contents of my stomach while on the bus.

When we arrived at the bus station in the centre of Santander, we were approached by a Spanish woman offering us accommodation for the night at a reasonable price. We followed her through the town expecting to be led to a guest house or hotel. Instead, we were taken to her tiny flat where we were shown where we were to spend the night. We declined her kind offer and went back into the town in search of a cheap hotel.

Fortunately, there were plenty of cheap hotels along the sea front and we quickly checked in and dropped off our bags. By now, the sun was beating down on us and my feelings of sickness had reappeared. 'We'll find a bar where you can get some food. That will settle your stomach down,' advised one of the Boro lads.

I didn't fancy any food, but thought if I got some substance in my belly, the acids would have something else to eat besides my stomach lining. We found a cafe bar and ordered some food and beer. The taste of the beer was only making me worse and when the food finally arrived, I jumped up and raced to the toilet. The toilet was pitch black and I didn't have time to find the light switch. I stood there, throwing up all over the toilet. The smell was horrendous, but as I couldn't see the sick, I just tried to blank it out. After a few moments, I thought I had been as sick as I could. Until that is, the chef walked in, turned on the light and saw the sick all over the tiled floor. This started me off again and my bout of sickness continued, much to the disgust of the Spaniard who left me to it.

The heavy bout of sickness cleared my head and I returned to the bar completely refreshed. By now, a couple of Chelsea fans from Tunbridge Wells had joined us. I recognised their faces from previous trips, and when they said they were with a mob of about 30 other Chelsea fans, we asked who they were. Sure enough, they were the usual faces from Chelsea that often follow England, and if they were in Santander, trouble was guaranteed. After a quick chat, the two Chelsea lads said they were going to some other bar to meet up with the rest of their firm. They invited us along, but we declined their offer and said we would see them later on at the ground.

We spent the rest of the afternoon walking from bar to bar along the sea front in the general direction of the ground, which was a couple of miles from the centre of town, along the coast road. The beaches in Santander were beautiful and packed with Spanish holiday makers. From time to time, we met a few other England fans, but up till then it had felt very different to any other England trip I had been on. There was none of the usual mobbing up and anti-social behaviour so loved by gangs of England fans abroad.

All that changed when we finally reached the ground. Once again we didn't have tickets for the game, but despite the lies that the FA had been spreading back home, tickets were readily available from the ticket office. There were small groups of England fans hanging around, but they were being closely observed by Spanish riot police. Nothing was happening, so we went through the turnstiles and into the ground. The ground was similar to Elland Road, circa 1988, and the English fans were allocated half of one of the ends behind a goal. There was a narrow terrace with seats behind and to our left was a four foot fence and right next to that was the home end, which was packed with Spanish teenagers vociferously chanting, 'Espana!'

My first instincts were that the segregation was completely inadequate to prevent the fans clashing inside the ground. However, I had not bargained on the sheer brutality of the Spanish police. Each time an England fan attempted to put up a Union flag, he was viciously assaulted by the riot police. There was no verbal warnings or polite requests for us to refrain from flying the flag of our nation. Each time the police dished out a beating, the Spanish crowd cheered. It seemed that they had come to watch England fans getting battered all night. The Spanish have a reputation for being cruel to animals, and on this occasion, the English fans were most definitely being treated like animals.

The game hadn't even kicked off, but numerous England fans had already been beaten black and blue by the police. I couldn't wait for the arrival of the Chelsea mob. They would not take this kind of treatment lying down, and perhaps if we all stuck together, we would be able to do something about it. The Chelsea boys did arrive in time to listen to the national anthem, but as *God Save The Queen* was played, the English fans who stood to sing the anthem were brutally attacked by police wielding batons. Throughout the game, every time an England fan stood up or tried to start singing, a mob of police would wade through the crowd, attack the offender until he was lying on the ground, and then leave him to nurse his bruises.

There was only about 700 England fans in our end and certainly not enough boys to do anything about the police brutality. One fan in particular seemed to enjoy getting beaten by the police. Each time he stood up, he was knocked down. Each time he started singing, he was battered. This continued every few minutes throughout the game. He genuinely seemed to be enjoying the pain. It reached a climax for him, probably in more ways than one, when he had the audacity to pretend to stick a Spanish flag up his arse. This infuriated the police so much, that they battered him unconscious. At no time did they make any attempt to arrest him.

At half-time, I went under the stand to get a drink. Further down the concourse, hundreds of Spanish fans were also getting their half-time refreshments. There was no effective segregation, just a line of riot police separating the Spanish fans from the English. Mobbing up near the refreshment bar were the 30 or so Chelsea boys who had spotted the ideal opportunity to attack this line of police and get to the Spanish fans at the same time.

They asked us if we were prepared to stand with them. I was all out for seeking revenge on the police for their cowardly behaviour on the terraces, but I was not very hopeful that our plan would succeed. There were hundreds of angry riot police in and around the ground, and if we did manage to beat the handful of police under the stand, there was no doubt that their colleagues would give us the beating of our lives. In addition, they would probably arrest us and God knows what would happen to us in the cells.

Out of loyalty to our nation though, we stood with the Chelsea boys and charged at the Spanish fans. As expected, the Spanish ran for their lives, but within seconds the riot police had launched a blistering counter attack. The Chelsea boys stood their ground and took a hell of a beating from the police. Eventually, we had to retreat and ran back on to the terraces. We had to climb a narrow staircase and waiting at the top of the stairs were more riot police. As we dodged the batons from behind, we had no choice but to run headlong into another attack, with more blows raining down on us from above. One of the Boro lads fell and was kicked, punched and hit with batons until he was unconscious. After what must have seemed like a life time to the Boro lad, the police eventually stopped hitting him. We picked him up and slapped him around until he regained consciousness.

Our attack on the police had only increased their anger and for the rest of the game, the police continually attacked the English fans. Some of the fans spotted some officials from the FA and asked them to do something about the treatment that was being dished out. The police obviously didn't know who they were, and they too were attacked. The FA officials were promising the fans that this treatment would be brought to the attention of top government officials back home. There was no way the Spanish authorities would be allowed to treat English citizens in this way.

Needless to say, I never heard anything about the events that took place that night when I returned home. The government was clearly of the opinion that anyone who watches England abroad deserves to be treated in the way we were. They were probably grateful to the Spanish for dishing out the beatings that the English police wouldn't be able to get away with. Members of the Football Intelligence Unit were also present at the game, but they didn't take any action to prevent the Spanish police attacking the England fans. Perhaps the English police were enjoying watching us get assaulted.

Apart from the Chelsea boys, there wasn't really any other mobs of England fans there. There were a few game lads from other clubs up and down the country, but the only decent mob of any size or quality was Chelsea. Most of the other fans were just normal supporters who had travelled on official FA trips. I don't think they expected this kind of treatment, and as they weren't hooligans, they had every right to expect the English police and the English FA to look out for their personal safety.

I couldn't wait for the end of the game so I could get away from the never ending onslaught from the police. When we left the ground, there were hundreds of Spanish fans waiting in the gravel park just behind our end. Most of them were just teenagers and their presence didn't worry me at all. We were with the Chelsea firm and it was clear that the Spanish, despite having the numbers, would put up as much of a fight as they had inside the ground. The police clearly realised there could be a potential flash point and slowly started walking towards the Spanish. The local youths were obviously used to the local police methods, and had no intention of being on the receiving end of the sort of punishment beatings we had received.

The Spanish fans quickly dispersed and with the majority of England fans boarding the official transport, it left the Chelsea fans and a few other little mobs at the mercy of the police. The Chelsea boys were well up for attacking the police, but fortunately, none of the others wanted to help them. In the end, the Chelsea boys decided to head down to the red light district to see if they could find any action with the local pimps and drug pushers.

The rest of us made our way back along the coast road towards the town centre. Police vans packed with riot police kept driving past, and I was starting to worry that they would pull over and arrest us on some trumped up charge. We came across a disco bar and decided to decamp in there until the police had left the area.

The disco was packed with young Spaniards and, as in Bilbao, our presence did not seem to concern them at all. After a few beers, we soon started to relax and the full extent of the horrific policing we had witnessed started to sink in. If any other group of Englishmen had been treated in the same way as we had been, the English media and government would have raised all sorts of human rights and civil liberty issues. Rightly so as well, but as it was only English football fans, we all knew the matter would be swiftly swept under the carpet. No doubt, a few British politicians would have been quite happy at the treatment dished out. I bet they had plenty to laugh about at their parties at the Spanish embassy anyway.

The disco music in this bar really was dreadful and after we had sunk a few beers, it really started getting on our nerves. The Spanish were loving it and the dance floor was packed with the local boys doing their best John Travolta impressions in front of the gullible Spanish girls. A couple of us approached the disc jockey to see if he would accept any dedications. Luckily, he spoke reasonable English and said we could look through his record collection to see if there was anything suitable.

There were hordes of records and none of us recognised any of the artists, but at the bottom of the pile was an old Madness album. He agreed to play the record for us and said it would come on in a few minutes. Suddenly, I started having visions of the brutal Spanish police bursting on to the dance floor and battering us, in a similar way the Sardinian police had in 1990.

When *Baggy Trousers* was played, time suddenly stood still. The Spanish stopped dancing and looked on in amazement. A few of them went to speak to the disc jockey to see what was going on. He was taking a lot of stick, but was clearly blaming us for the choice in music. We thought we better make a point and made our way to the dance floor.

A few Madness songs were played from the album, but by the time side one had finished, the disco was virtually empty. The disc jockey started playing the Spanish music once again, but by now the majority of customers had left the club. And when it became clear that he wouldn't play any more of our music, we also left and returned to our hotel.

In the morning, we woke up early and walked down to the bus station. A couple of English lads told us that the Chelsea boys had been fighting in the town the previous night, and had all ended up getting arrested. I wasn't sure if the lad was telling the truth, but if he was, I felt sorry for the Chelsea lads and was pleased that we hadn't gone off with them after the game. Mind you, it probably wouldn't have been classed as a good trip for them unless they had ended up in a police cell.

Holland, 1993

AFTER THE FRIENDLY in Spain, England concentrated on qualifying for the 1994 World Cup to be held in the USA. Our qualifying group consisted of San Marino, Norway, Poland and Holland. England were so confident of qualifying for the final stages of the tournament that they organised a close season tour of America in the summer of 1993. They were to play the USA in Boston and Germany in Detroit.

As far as I was concerned, Holland was the trip everyone had to go on. Most English fans were fed up with hearing about how tough the Dutch were supposed to be. We had played in London, Düsseldorf and Sardinia, and at none of these games had we come across anything that even resembled a mob of casual hooligans. There would be no excuses for the Dutch if they failed to appear in Rotterdam or Amsterdam.

As well as the Holland game, I also fancied going to Norway, Poland and San Marino, but the thought of visiting America was the main attraction. At the cost of missing out on the trips to the other three away games in Europe, I booked up a trip to North America. I was only interested in going to Detroit to watch the Germany game, but as we didn't fancy spending a week in Detroit, we flew to Toronto instead. We intended to drive to Detroit for the game, but in the end we never made it, and spent a week sampling the delights of Toronto.

When we returned from our trip to Canada, we booked up for the trip to Holland. Instead of flying to Amsterdam, we decided to fly to Düsseldorf on the Saturday before the game. The plan was to spend Saturday night in Germany and then catch a train to Amsterdam on the Sunday. We would base ourselves in Amsterdam until the Thursday, when we would return home, via Düsseldorf. The game was to be played in Rotterdam on the Wednesday night and was an easy train journey from Amsterdam.

Four of us made the trip and arrived in Düsseldorf on Saturday around lunch time. We met a few other England fans on the flight who had the same idea as us, except they were spending the Saturday night in Cologne. We left the other lads at the airport and caught a train into Düsseldorf. It was my first visit to Düsseldorf, although the area near the train station was familiar to me from news footage of the clashes during the European Championships in 1988.

The square opposite the station was full of Turkish lads, which caused us to be a little edgy as we all remembered how dangerous the Turks had been in Berlin and Malmo. We walked all around the town, in search of accommodation, but at every hotel we received the same story. 'Sorry, no vacancies.'

It struck me that the English were not too popular in Düsseldorf. After about an hour or so, someone told us to visit the tourist information office near the train station as they would do the searching for us. Sure enough, a few telephone calls were made and a room for the night was booked. When we turned up at the hotel, the landlord told us we were not welcome, but as we had already paid a deposit he was in no position to turn us away.

We were keen to sample some more German beer, but on a Saturday afternoon, Düsseldorf resembled a ghost town. The streets were deserted and the shops were shut. It was very mysterious and none of us could figure out what was going on. However, when we came across the first pub, it was full to the brim with Germans, drinking and singing. We hadn't realised, but German shops shut early on Saturday and it appeared that the rest of the day was spent getting pissed. It sounded like a wonderful idea to me and we were only too happy to join in with the locals. After all, when in Rome and all that.

Each time we ordered a beer, we were served a tiny glass with a creamy, dark liquid. It appeared to be our equivalent of bitter and was a bit of an acquired taste. We were gulping these beers down and laughing at the Germans who were slowly sipping their beers. We were underestimating the power of the local brew though, and after an hour or so we were getting really pissed. We started discussing the beer with one of the Germans who expressed his surprise that we weren't drinking lager. He advised us to order Pilsner, so the rest of the day was spent drinking Pilsner lager.

Nigel Benn was fighting Chris Eubank that night and we were hoping to find a bar that would be showing the big fight on television. We were not to be disappointed, and the Alstadt was packed with hundreds of bars, many of which were showing the fight. We ended up in an Irish bar which was packed with English lads who were working in the building game over in Germany. We were all well pissed as we watched the boxing and then headed on to a night club.

The Germans weren't particularly friendly, but no one gave us any hassle at all during the night. I ended up back in the hotel room, asleep on the springs of the bed, with the heavy mattress on top of me. I slept like a log, but awoke in the morning with indentations all over my back and yet another nasty hangover.

We didn't bother buying tickets for the train to Amsterdam, but we were soon clobbered by the train guard and forced to pay for the journey. We spent the journey discussing the previous night's drunken antics and speculating as to what we would discover in Rotterdam and Amsterdam.

The newspapers back home had claimed that no alcohol would be sold in Rotterdam on the day of the game in a bid to keep the fans sober, thus minimising the risk of trouble. I said to the others that we shouldn't get to Rotterdam too early on Wednesday because of the beer ban in the town.

One of the other lads replied, 'I know how we'll get around that. We just won't drink in Rotterdam.' He seemed quite pleased with the idea that he had pulled a fast one on the Dutch authorities. If they won't serve us beer, we'll teach them a lesson by not drinking any.

A little later on, we were discussing the team for the big game. 'I hope that John Barnes doesn't play, I can't stand him', I observed.

'Yeah, thirty grand a week he earns. What a waste of taxpayers' money.'

Once again, the same lad. I think the German beer was too much for him, but luckily he didn't say much for the rest of the journey.

We arrived in Amsterdam on Sunday afternoon and had no trouble finding accommodation. We were literally dragged off the train by a young Dutch lad, who promised to take us to the most luxurious hotel in Amsterdam for what sounded like very reasonable room rates. When we reached the hotel, we discovered why the rooms were so cheap. The place was a hovel, but we weren't too bothered. It was a place to dump your luggage and have a shower. On the plus side, it was cheap and right in the heart of the red light district.

The rest of the day was spent getting accustomed to Amsterdam and its various attractions. The girls in the shop windows kept us amused, but none of us really wanted to risk getting a dose from some old tart. However, their posing did keep us entertained and plenty of English lads were only too happy to employ their services. Drugs were also readily available on the street and in the cafe bars, but I was more interested in the lager. Unfortunately, Amstel and Heineken is not up to the standards set in Germany and Czechoslovakia, and the price of a drink in Amsterdam was fairly high. Despite this, the lager did its job and we spent the rest of the day getting pissed.

As usual, there were plenty of English tourists in Amsterdam and their numbers were increased by hundreds of casually dressed young lads who were there for the football. The Grasshoppers bar opposite the main train station appeared to be the focal point for the English fans, with large groups of fans meeting there throughout the day.

All day, we kept on hearing rumours that a mob of Ajax fans would be roaming the streets in search of the English. One thing you soon learn at football is take all these stories with a pinch of salt. Quite often, some idiot will make up a story in an attempt to look wise or hard. Even though it was probably yet another fabricated story, we stuck together, keen to ensure that a large and reliable mob was ready to confront the Ajax fans if indeed the rumours turned out to be true.

Just down the road from the Grasshoppers was a huge pub, with three different floors and loud music. This was soon packed with English fans and we spent the next few hours drinking in there. After that, we went on a pub crawl. We were in one bar when we were approached by a middle aged Dutch man. He came over and declared, 'I must tell you that the Dutch are eternally grateful to the English nation for defeating the Germans in the war. I must buy you a beer.'

We took him up on his kind offer and even explained that none of us had taken an active role in the war. This didn't deter him and we had a drink with him and listened enthusiastically as he proceeded to slag off the Germans. Every now and then we even joined in with him. As we were chatting to the grateful Dutch man, a group of younger Dutch lads came over to us and asked us if we were England fans. They didn't look menacing and certainly didn't appear to be aggressive. However, all of us were prepared for the possibility of a fight. 'Yeah, we're English, are you Ajax?' we replied in a confrontational manner.

I felt a little embarrassed at the provocative stance we had adopted, when a Dutch lad replied, 'Do you want to take on Holland at table football?'

We laughed and relaxed a little, and agreed to take them on. We went to the bar to get more drinks and to get some change for the machine and started boasting to them about how we were going to whip their arses and how this would be a warm up for the big game on Wednesday. We had to demonstrate to these Dutch fairies that England was a better nation than Holland in all respects.

We were quietly confident as well, until the game started. Our tactics revolved around us spinning our players until they connected with the ball, and hoping that we would be able to connect with the ball well enough for a goal to be scored. Their tactics, on the other hand, appeared to have been meticulously devised at the famous Ajax youth academy. They were passing it, dummying it, playing offside and doing overhead kicks. At one stage, one of their players went on a run beating four men before slipping it past our goalkeeper. I think the Dutch went on to win each of the ten games by nine goals to nil.

We took defeat in typically gracious style. 'You won't be so fucking clever when we turn you lot over on Wednesday and smash up your country.'

The Dutch lads laughed off our threats, bought us another drink, and discussed the big game in a more reasonable manner than us.

We continued our crawl through Amsterdam and stumbled upon what appeared to be a violent incident. A mob of Leicester City fans were surrounded by police outside a bar. From what I could hear, they had been involved in some sort of dispute, but none of us really had any interest in getting involved with them. They all looked fairly young, and drugs were no doubt the primary reason for their bravado.

We were sat in one bar when we noticed a vast number of girls going into a night club opposite our bar. There were hundreds of them and many of them were very pretty, so we decided to join them. Unfortunately, the bouncers wouldn't let us in, explaining that it because we had trainers on rather than shoes. A likely excuse. We returned to the bar where the barman told us that we had actually been refused admission because we clearly weren't lesbians.

It had been a long day, and we had all had enough beer. We made our way back to our hotel in the middle of the red light district. Most of the English fans had failed to venture any further than this area and it looked like the girls in the shop windows were doing a roaring trade. One of our lads was quite tempted to employ the services of a big black girl who had caught his eye as she played with herself in the window. We urged him on and he walked towards the window. The girl saw him coming and made gestures with her hands clearly indicating that she wasn't interested. 'Look lads, she don't even want paying.'

Needless to say, she didn't want paying because she didn't want fucked by a drunken Englishman who had spent the last 48 hours drinking lager and eating chips.

It had been a good night out. There were plenty of English fans around, but apart from taking drugs, drinking too much, and shagging prostitutes, most of them had behaved themselves. We had no bother with the notorious Ajax hooligans and all the Dutch people we met were warm and welcoming. However, we knew more and more English fans would be arriving over the next couple of days and as the big game approached, tensions would increase and trouble would be inevitable.

Monday was spent drinking in the two large bars near the main train station. These bars had become the central meeting point for the English and you could sit there and enjoy the drink while watching more fans arriving in Amsterdam by rail. On more than one occasion, we noticed our hotel tout showing other English lads to the most luxurious hotel in Amsterdam.

As more and more English fans arrived the possibility of violence increased. In addition, more and more police were taking to the streets, hoping their presence would be enough to deter the English from kicking it off. However, when you stick so many English lads in a city like Amsterdam with its abundant supply of vices, there is only ever going to be one outcome. It really was a recipe for disaster.

The bars were packed on the Monday night and the atmosphere was certainly a lot different to the relaxed atmosphere of the Sunday night. A lot of England fans were drinking in the streets outside the three storey pub we were in. They were closely monitored by the police and were revelling in the attention. The usual drunken chants of patriotism and anger echoed round the streets. 'No surrender to the IRA!', *Rule Britannia*, and the all time favourite, *God Save The Queen*.

There is nothing wrong with singing football songs of course, but the media always has a go at the England fans for doing so, claiming that we do nothing but bring shame on our country. They often claim that all England fans are racist neo-Nazis, but we must live in the only country in the world where anyone showing any hint of patriotism is branded like that. Tell me, what is so wrong with singing your national anthem or chanting defiant songs about a terrorist organisation that frequently murders women and children? Perhaps the Government are frightened of the England fan who is proud of his country and its history and who detests the thought of self-confessed terrorists being invited into the House of Commons or Downing Street to take tea with the Prime Minister. The Government certainly appears to be more scared of a few drunken English fans enjoying themselves abroad than they do of the likes of Gerry Adams. They certainly seem to waste more time and money trying to prevent people travelling abroad than they do on protecting the safety of loyal British subjects left at the mercy of terrorists in places such as Belfast.

There was actually no need for the group of fans to be outside as the pub was huge and could easily accommodate all the drinkers. The police were trying to push the fans back into the bar, when, surprise surprise, someone threw a bottle. The police were quick to react and charged the fans into the bar, hitting anyone that wasn't fast enough to get through the doors. As the English ran inside, they made sure they threw their remaining bottles at the police.

We now found ourselves in a siege situation. The pub was surrounded by riot police and inside were hundreds of drunken Englishmen, armed with bottles, glasses and pool balls. It was going to take a very shrewd man to negotiate a peaceful settlement. As far as I could see, there was only one possible outcome. A violent confrontation culminating in the mass deportation of hundreds of English men. My fears only escalated when I had a look out of the back door of the pub. I thought this might offer a way out, but when a few of us carefully peered out, we discovered it led into a dark alley. When you looked left and right, you could see hundreds of police just waiting for the English to try to escape.

For a while, the bar continued to serve alcohol, but eventually, the police sent in one of their leading negotiators. He ordered the pub to stop serving alcohol and announced that we should all drink up and quietly leave the bar. I thought he would be leading us into a trap, but to be fair, he was as good as his word and when we left the pub, the police didn't try to attack us or arrest us. They had dealt with a potentially explosive situation in a very capable manner.

However, the English fans were still hyped up and the old rumours concerning mobs of Ajax fans started circulating once again. The mob of English fans stuck together and started to wander off in search of the elusive Ajax hooligans. Every now and then we came across small groups of English fans who told us how they had been fighting with mobs of Ajax fans tooled up with gas and sharpened umbrellas. Whether their claims were true or not, I don't know, but the police followed us everywhere we went and were successful in splitting us up into smaller groups.

I gave up the chase and returned to a quiet bar near my hotel. Shortly after I had settled down with a beer, the sound of sirens could be heard. Perhaps the English had found the Ajax fans after all. I really couldn't be bothered with it anymore and spent the rest of the evening chatting and drinking. There were a few Australian girls in this bar who I recognised as they were also staying in our hotel. We were chatting to them, but seeing as they were drinking more than us and we couldn't keep up, it seemed highly unlikely that we would pull them.

Tuesday was spent in much the same way as Sunday and Monday. Amsterdam is a beautiful city with many attractions for tourists. However, when travelling with England, most of these attractions simply do not interest the average England fan. Who would want to do such mundane things as visit an art gallery or go on a boat trip when there are more important things to do, such as drinking, chatting, and for many people taking drugs and shagging prostitutes.

It was a relaxing day as we mellowed out in the various bars and cafes in the centre of the town. By now, Amsterdam was packed with England fans and the possibility of violence erupting later on that night was very real. But for now, most of the fans were enjoying the calm before the storm.

We had three options to pass the time if we didn't want to spend all day and all night drinking and generally socialising while getting as pissed as possible. In the evening, The Buzzcocks were playing a gig and quite a few people wanted to go to see them play. Other lads were keen on visiting some of the numerous pornographic cinemas dotted throughout Amsterdam. The most attractive option as far as I was concerned though was to make the short trip over to Utrecht to watch the under-21s play. None of us had tickets for the big game the following day, and from what I could see, neither did any of the other England fans. I felt that as I had made the effort to come over to Holland, it would be nice to see some football. Also, the thought of leaving Amsterdam for a few hours was increasingly appealing. It is a fine city, but as I was not interested in buying sex or drugs or rock n' roll, the attractions on offer to me in Amsterdam were limited.

We decided to go to Utrecht and walked up to the station to jump the train over to the game. On arrival in Utrecht, we were unsure as to what we would find. There was always the possibility that Dutch firms from all over the country would firm up here, watch the game, and then travel into Amsterdam after the game to confront the English. I had read in the papers back home, that Utrecht was one of the many Dutch teams who were supposed to have an organised firm of hooligans. Certainly, although I was glad to be out of Amsterdam for a few hours, we were in no position to relax our guard.

It was only a short journey and in no time at all we had arrived in Utrecht. The area around the station was fairly quiet and although a few other England fans had jumped off our train, the small police presence did not appear to be too concerned at the arrival of the England fans. We left the other English lads and strolled off into the town in search of a bar. It was a strange town because we were unable to find many shops or bars, and the streets were virtually deserted.

Our search led us to the football ground, a good few hours before kick-off. The idea was to have a drink in the supporters bar. All the Dutch people we had met had been friendly and very hospitable, and the thought of spending a couple of hours drinking and chatting to some Dutch fans about football was quite appealing. The English lads were great, but as most of them were constantly under the influence of illegal substances, a lot of the conversations were tiresome and repetitive.

We purchased some tickets for the game and walked round the ground to the supporters bar. The ground was a good standard, similar to what you might expect these days in the first division in England. Unfortunately, the supporters bar was not quite up to scratch. Basically, it was just a cafe, and although it served alcohol, it wasn't the most riveting place to spend soaking up the atmosphere of big time international football. We didn't really have the time to go off in search of livelier bars though, and so made the best of a bad situation by playing draughts. It was a strange build up to an England away game.

The time soon passed (not!), and we noticed the area around the ground filling up with Dutch football fans. Once again, all the Dutch fans were dressed head to toe in bright orange regalia. Many were wearing ridiculous hats and were playing musical instruments. The Dutch seem to treat each international game like a carnival, with whole families dressing up and enjoying the occasion. It certainly isn't my idea of the best way to watch football, but you have to hand it to the Dutch. They clearly enjoy themselves so who are we to moan?

What I do find funny is the stories that the English media make up about Dutch hooligans each time we have to play them in an international game. There is no doubt that disturbances do take place at league games in Holland, but at internationals? The only time I have ever heard of there being trouble at a Holland international match is on the occasions they play the Germans. Even then, the trouble is usually orchestrated by the Germans. It seems to me that the press like to portray the Dutch as crazier than the English, safe in the knowledge that a lot of the English fans will rise to the bait and take on the Dutch in an effort to prove that England still has the best hooligans.

The reason the press stoke up trouble in this way? Who knows, but one thing for sure is that Amsterdam was packed with English journalists who were there with the sole intention of reporting any outbreaks of trouble. They were lapping up the drugs, prostitutes and alcohol, all expenses reimbursed by their employers no doubt. If there was no possibility of trouble, there would be no need for them to be sent over to cover England games and therefore no opportunity for them to drink and shag their way round Europe at no personal expense.

We walked through the partying Dutch fans and into the end set aside exclusively for the England fans. There were quite a few there as well, although I don't know where they had been before the game. One thing I am sure of though is that none of them had spent the previous two hours playing draughts.

Andy Cole was playing for England and many of the Geordies had travelled to watch the game to cheer on their hero. He had a nightmare, missing chance after chance. To be honest, I can't remember the score, but it was an enjoyable game played to the back drop of a colourful and noisy crowd. There was no trouble in or around the ground, and afterwards we were escorted back to the station to catch the train back to Amsterdam.

When we arrived in Amsterdam at about eleven o'clock, the atmosphere was in stark contrast to the one in Utrecht. The large square opposite the station was packed with police vans. The sound of sirens filled the air and in the distance you could hear the sound of it kicking off. Apart from the police and the English fans, the streets were virtually deserted.

We managed to avoid getting stopped by the police outside the station and headed in the direction of the red light district. After just a few moments, we stumbled across a huge mob of English fans and were quickly put in the picture. A mob of Ajax fans had turned up and trouble had soon started. For the last hour or so, the English fans had been rampaging through the streets of Amsterdam, closely followed by the local police. There had been countless baton charges and quite a few English fans had been arrested.

The police were just behind this mob, and without warning launched another attack on us as we stood around talking. They just seemed to want to disperse the English into small groups, and from what I had heard, their intention was then to round up the English and arrest or deport them if they did not have tickets for the game the following evening. This seemed a bit of a liberty to me. Throughout the year, thousands of English tourists visit Amsterdam, and although England were playing Holland that week, not all the English people in Amsterdam were there solely to watch the football. However, these tourists risked deportation simply for being English. I later read that over 1,200 English people were deported from Holland and another 200 arrested that week, many just for not having tickets for the game.

In lots of cases, fans did have tickets for the games, safely locked away back at their hotels, but because they were not in possession of a match ticket when they were apprehended by the police, they were treated as criminals. Can you imagine the outcry if England played Holland at Wembley, and the English police went round the West End searching for Dutch tourists and deporting them if they didn't have tickets on their person for the game? It is a situation that would never happen in England, but something that often happens to Englishmen abroad. If you are deported from a country, it can have devastating consequences for a law abiding citizen, but it appears that foreign police are encouraged to deploy these tactics by our Government who are just not interested in hearing the full story.

The baton charges, bottle throwing, and fighting had already been going on for over two hours by the time we returned from Utrecht. With so many fans already arrested, the number of English lads out on the street was dwindling, and the police were slowly starting to take control of the situation. They had baton charged us into a narrow side street, in the heart of the red light district. They appeared to temporarily give up their assault and stood at the end of the street watching us to see what our next move would be.

The mob of English took their opportunity. About 100 of us charged down this street in the direction of a handful of police officers who were stood at the other end of the street. Without hesitation, they turned on their heels and ran for their lives. We now found ourselves directly outside a small police station. The front of the building was all glass and inside were two or three policemen stood behind a desk. Within seconds, bicycles and rubbish bins were picked up and launched through the windows, smashing the glass and sending the officers inside scurrying under their desks.

I realised we were now in a very serious situation and couldn't see how we were going to get out of it. The handful of police at the end of the street had now regrouped with quite a few of their colleagues. They charged up the street towards us. Now it was our turn to run, but to where? At the other end of the street were the riot police who had chased us down here in the first place. As expected, they were waiting for us and we now found ourselves trapped.

I found myself outside a small bar and rushed through the door in a bid to reach safety. Quite a few of the other lads had the same idea and the bar now found itself under siege from dozens of English fans desperate to escape imminent arrest. The bar staff tried in vain to keep us out of the bar, but fortunately, I managed to push my way in. Those left outside, were not so lucky and I can only assume they were some of the 200 English fans arrested that night in Amsterdam.

For me, my escape was still not complete. The police knew that dozens of us had forced our way into this bar and were bound to come in to look for us. I was on my own as I had been split up from my friends, but quickly realised that some of my fellow escapees were Carlisle boys. I didn't know any of them personally, but knew enough to realise they were all good boys. Carlisle have always

118

taken good numbers to England games and on the occasions I have stood alongside them, they have never let anyone down. This boosted my confidence a little, but I still wanted to escape. I knew my hotel was only a short walk away and if I could escape the attention of the police, I could be in the safety of my hotel bar within five minutes.

I went to the toilet and noticed a door leading to a back yard. There was a six foot high wall and I jumped up to see what was on the other side. All I could see was police and it was obvious that they would spot me if I tried to jump over. I sat down and thought for a few moments, but was still undecided. I returned to the bar, which was now packed with police. They were questioning the Carlisle boys and so I quietly went and stood in the far corner of the bar, pretending to be in a world of my own. Fortunately, someone had left a bottle of lager on the bar and although it was nearly empty, I stood there with it, pretending I had been in here all night.

The Carlisle boys were dragged out of the bar while the other police officers looked around the bar to see if they could see any other England fans. I felt like I was in the scene from *The Great Escape* when the German guards were checking the ID of the English lads on the train. Under my breath, I practised my best Dutch accent in case I was questioned, but fortunately the police left the bar without me.

I ordered a beer and started to relax a little. I still had to make the short walk back to the hotel and knew full well that the police were still nicking ticketless Englishmen. I remained in this bar for nearly an hour before deciding that I had no option but to risk taking to the streets. I kept my head down and walked hurriedly to my hotel. The police were still on the streets in large numbers, but luckily they ignored me.

We woke early on Wednesday and took to the streets to find out exactly what had happened the night before. So many rumours were flying around about arrests, injuries, and mass deportation that you could not be sure what was true unless you had seen it with your own eyes. One rumour I heard that did sound quite plausible was the story that the police were refusing to allow English fans on the train to Rotterdam unless they presented a match ticket before boarding. We had originally planned to stay in Amsterdam until late afternoon and then all travel on to Rotterdam together. I didn't want to risk this now and so we decided to catch an early train to Rotterdam.

Sure enough, there were dozens of police hanging around the main entrance to the station and in the ticket office area. Whether they were indeed checking tickets or not I didn't know, but I was not prepared to risk it. We walked further down the road outside the station and then jumped over the wall on to one of the platforms. We found out what platform the Rotterdam train was departing from and quietly sat in a waiting room until departure time. We didn't bother buying a ticket, but unfortunately the guard came round shortly after we left Amsterdam and so we had no option but to pay for the trip. Still, I wasn't that bothered. At least I was safely on the train and heading to Rotterdam. The hustle and bustle of Amsterdam could be left behind for a few hours while we sampled the delights on offer in another Dutch city.

The three of us relaxed on the train and after a little while we found ourselves dozing off. The events of the previous night had obviously taken their toll on our bodies. I woke up a little later and noticed that the train had come to a halt in a station. I looked out of the window to my left and noticed that we had stopped at Den Haag. I said to my mate, 'They're supposed to have a bit of a firm.'

I turned to my right and was horrified to see the platform packed with hundreds of Dutch fans. And this time, they were not the usual clowns dressed all in orange. They were all blokes in their late teens and early twenties. They weren't wearing any colours, but they were hardly what you would call well dressed either. Their idea of fashion seemed to consist of shell suits and loud trainers. They looked like poorly dressed Scousers from the late Seventies.

They boarded the train and walked down our carriage. They were boisterous and plenty of them were carrying bottles. I was sure they would spot that we were English and take the opportunity to hurt us. As they walked past, I pretended to be asleep but still expected to get a hiding any second. To be fair, they did the decent thing and ignored us, but we now realised that we would be in a tricky situation when we arrived in Rotterdam. There were bound to be mobs of England fans drinking outside the station and as soon they saw hundreds of Dutch hooligans, it would inevitably kick off. Our problem was the fact that we would be with the Dutch fans coming off the trains. I didn't fancy getting caught up in this battle if the English thought I was Dutch. Although they had the numbers, the Dutch didn't look too clued up to me. I suspected that they would bottle it when confronted by a mob of English lads.

When the train arrived in Rotterdam I was surprised to see so few police at the station. The Dutch mob got off, while we waited on the train. They firmed up and appeared to be leaving the station by a back exit. I didn't know where they were going, but took the opportunity to get out of the station and find the rest of the English fans. There was a couple of bars just down the road from the station and despite the propaganda in the media, all were serving alcohol. There were only a few other England fans in these bars and when we told them that a couple of hundred Dutch hooligans had just arrived in Rotterdam, we all knew that we were in danger. We had to find a decent sized mob of English fans so that we could put up a fight against the Dutch, otherwise we were liable for a serious pasting.

We left the bars by the station and headed into the town where we came across a huge square, with shops and offices surrounding a large, concrete concourse. It certainly didn't resemble the square we discovered in Czechoslovakia and wouldn't appear in any holiday brochures, but there were a few bars in the area and the square was really the ideal place for two mobs to confront each other.

We ordered a beer in a bar where a few more English were drinking. By now, there was about 15 of us and we all knew that hundreds of Dutch fans had just left the station and were on the look out for England fans. We stood outside the bar, keeping our glasses, bottles, chairs and tables within easy reach, just in case.

After a few minutes, we heard a loud bang, like the sound of an explosive device being let off. This was quickly followed by the unmistakable sound of it kicking off. We could hear glasses smashing and the sound of people shouting at each other. We knew it was kicking off, but couldn't see where or what exactly was happening. It was obviously kicking off down one of the side streets leading off from the square. We tooled up and expected the worst. Our fears came true when we suddenly saw over 200 Dutch fans charging towards us from across the other side of the square. They still had about 100 yards to cover before they reached our bar, but we all knew what we were going to do.

We picked up our weapons and charged at them. We were heavily outnumbered and probably didn't stand a chance, but we were not going to run from the Dutch at all costs. It was an incredible display of loyalty because you have to remember that we had only met our brothers in arms just a few minutes earlier. We

121

didn't even know what team they supported, but one thing we all shared in common was our loyalty and pride in England.

I can't remember what was going through my head as I waited for the Dutch fans to reach me, but I knew I would shortly be getting a severe beating. There weren't even any police in the area. As the Dutch fans got within spitting distance of us, they turned and ran to their left. I couldn't believe they were dropping their bottle from us and as it turned out I was right. As they turned to their left and continued running, behind them I could see hundreds of English fans who had been chasing the Dutch fans. Suddenly, we were now in an even more precarious situation.

The English mob had failed to follow the Dutch and were now heading straight at our small mob, stood outside the bar armed with chairs and bottles. Frantically we shouted at them, 'We're English!', and luckily, our screams alerted the boys at the front who stopped charging towards us.

We recognised a few of the faces at the front of the mob, lads from Boro and Aston Villa. 'You fucking cunts,' yelled one of the Villa boys. 'You're the only fucking mob that has stood all day.'

The pleasantries soon ended, and we still had the little matter of catching up with the Dutch fans. We all turned and charged towards where the Dutch fans had run to. They were certainly a lot fitter than the English and we didn't stand a chance of catching them. We gave up the chase fairly quickly and I was brought up to date with what had happened.

The English had been drinking in a few bars opposite each other in a side street just off the square when the Dutch fans arrived. The Dutch threw a home made nail bomb at the English and fired an air pistol into the crowd, hitting an English lad in the leg. Once they had used their weapons, the English charged into them. Although a few punches were thrown, the Dutch turned and ran towards us.

This was a huge mob of England lads. All were casually dressed and many were boys from some of the top firms in the country. While I was busy renewing old acquaintances, the rest of the lads were determined to go and find the Dutch mob. Just as we were setting off to find them, hundreds of police converged on the square from all four directions.

'Stand and fight!' urged some of the Chelsea and Queens Park Rangers fans.

A lot of the English were up for it at first, but you soon realised that the police had swamped the area. We really didn't stand a chance as slowly the police surrounded us on all four sides and herded us into the centre of the square.

We were kept in this position for a good 30 minutes without receiving any information as to what was to happen to us. Eventually, a police officer with a loud hailer addressed the crowd. 'Buses will shortly arrive to take you to the stadium. You will be allowed to pay to get into the ground. Refreshments will be available.'

It sounded quite reasonable to me. Hardly any of us had tickets for the game, and at least this way we would all be guaranteed admission. However, quite wisely, a lot of the lads didn't believe the promises that were being made. The Chelsea and QPR lads in particular were all still for fighting their way out of the square, finding the Dutch mob, and battering them. The promises from the police had cast doubts in other people's minds though, and a lot of the lads were undecided as to whether to trust the police or continue causing trouble. The doubts meant that the mob was divided and consequently not as powerful as before.

We didn't stand a chance of escaping from the square unless we acted as one single unit. Buses were brought up to the square and the fans were all escorted on to them. Once all the buses were loaded up, we set off in convoy, supposedly to the ground.

Now that we were safely on the buses, the Dutch suddenly had the bravery to return to the area. Up near the train station, more trouble erupted. The police were too busy guarding us and couldn't leave the buses to quell the disorder. Had they done so, we would have escaped and they would have had even more problems on their hands. As it turned out, the hundreds of Dutch fans came a little unstuck as a smaller number of England fans gave it to the them. Apparently, many of these boys were from Oxford, and they certainly gave us something to cheer about from the safety of our buses.

The behaviour of the English fans in Rotterdam was widely condemned by the English media. However, from my point of view, I felt nothing but pride for my country and all the people who stood together. A nail bomb was thrown at us and a Dutch fan fired a gun at us. What do the newspapers expect us to do? Bow down and surrender? I for one am proud of the way we stood together and attacked the Dutch hooligans. This was not a group of innocent Dutch families getting bullied by drunken English yobs. This was a mob of well organised and tooled up Dutch lads, intent on killing some England fans. This may sound a little over dramatic, but when it comes down to it, if you use bombs and guns someone will indeed die one day. Just a few years later, a Dutch fan was killed in a battle between rival gangs of Ajax and Feyenoord supporters. We might be condemned as mindless morons, but sometimes you have no alternative but to fight. I appreciate that fighting is wrong, but I live in the real world and am wise enough to realise that sometimes you have no alternative but to fight to protect yourself.

So called 'genuine' football fans may disagree with me. They should consider this. If England fans were enjoying a party in Rotterdam and were attacked by a gang of Dutch hooligans armed with explosives and firearms, who would protect the law abiding fan? Certainly not the police. All they are ever interested in doing is arresting, deporting and assaulting England fans without giving a second thought as to whether they may be innocent or not. You could argue that if English hooligans were not in Holland, then the Dutch fans would not have been so aggressive. Yes, in an ideal world there would be no hooligans in either country and everyone would live in peace. But this is not an ideal world, and hooliganism and violence do exist, not only in England, but in every country in the world. In situations such as this, it is the so called hooligans that protect the innocent fan who does not wish to or cannot stand up for himself.

The buses drove away from the town centre and some of the lads started recognising the area. They had travelled in the opposite direction when arriving in the town from the port. We realised the game was up and genuinely believed the police were taking us straight to the ferry to be deported back to England in shame and at the mercy of the tabloid press.

The possibility of getting deported didn't really bother me that much. My main concern was my passport and baggage that was still in my hotel in Amsterdam. I would have to try to obtain another passport and then return to Amsterdam to collect my luggage. All this hassle and for what? We get threatened by a mob of Dutch, we stand our ground, and suddenly we're the criminals.

As it turned out, there wasn't a ferry in the port so we were taken to a military barracks to be detained until such time as a ferry was prepared to take us. The buses parked up in a large exercise yard, but we were not allowed to leave them. A constant armed guard of police and soldiers saw to that. There was nothing we could do and we just sat on the buses for hours, furious with ourselves for falling for such an obvious trick. I was lucky in that I knew a lot of the boys on our bus from previous trips, and it was nice to see these lads and catch up on the gossip.

After a few hours, tempers started to flare. All of us had been drinking prior to being taken into custody and a lot of us were desperate for a piss. Kick-off time was also approaching and those that had tickets for the game were going mad at the possibility of missing it. Things were obviously still going on in the town centre or near the ground, as by now most of the police had left the compound, leaving just the young soldiers and a handful of police to guard us.

A few naive guards bowed to the pressure and allowed us to leave the bus, one by one, to take a piss up the side of the bus. When the doors were opened, all of us stood up and surged through them. The soldiers didn't stand a chance and as we overpowered them, so too did the English on the other buses. Once out of the bus, I ran to a fence with about half a dozen other lads. We yanked at it until it started to collapse. Just as it was about to tumble over, I saw three or four police officers running towards us. With one final push, the fence tumbled over and we were off.

The compound was surrounded on three sides by vast playing fields and we raced across them, closely followed by the police. At one stage, the police nearly caught me, but I managed to break away from their clutches. We ran across the fields, jumping over narrow streams, until we could run no more. Tired and out of breath, we stopped running and turned around to see the police had given up the chase. I was pleased, but also concerned because only about six of us had managed to escape. I assumed the rest of the English lads had been prevented from making good their escape, and thought that they would probably now be charged with some criminal offence, rather than just be deported. In addition, if there was only half a dozen escapees, the police would be on to us in an instant.

By now, it was getting dark and we really couldn't go back the way we had come. In the distance, we could see some lights and what looked like a road. We headed in that direction, but after a while our path was blocked by a wall. We climbed over the wall and found ourselves at the start of an army style assault course. There was no other way out so we had no alternative but to take on the obstacles. After a few minutes of climbing over walls and jumping over ditches, we eventually reached the end of the assault course.

125

Our final obstacle was a 10 feet high wall. Once over the wall, we would be back out in the streets. We spotted a tree and climbed up it, eased our way along a branch that was leaning over the wall, and dropped to the floor. All of us completed our escape safely.

We now found ourselves in a deserted road, with steep banks of grass on either side. On the other side of the road was the estuary leading into the North Sea. On the other side of the water, the floodlights from the stadium lit up the area. It was very nearly kick-off time and the noise of the crowd could easily be heard in the distance. As the crow flies, the ground was probably less than half a mile away. The only thing stopping us reaching the ground in time for kick-off was the busiest shipping lane in the world.

We walked down to the shore and spotted a little rowing boat. A few of the lads fancied the idea of rowing across the freezing water to the other side. As we discussed the chances of successfully navigating the crossing, a huge North Sea ferry came in to sight. The thought of colliding with that beast scuppered our daft plans.

We started walking along the road, but knew the police would soon be on our tails. Every time a car approached, we ran down the grass banks and hid behind trees. A helicopter was soon hovering in the sky above us, directing a spotlight onto the ground below. After a few minutes, about a dozen Dutch guys appeared out of nowhere in the road ahead of us.

It looked like we had a fight on our hands, so we took the usual stance. Arms out wide, chest out. 'Come on then!' we yelled.

'Stop! Armed police!' came the reply.

My heart skipped a beat when I saw their revolvers. They ordered us to put our hands above our heads and marched us to a fence by the side of the road. We were handcuffed and told to wait quietly, while they returned to their car to obtain further orders. A couple of them kept a watch on us. In the distance, the sound of the English fans singing God Save The Queen could easily be heard, wafting over the sea. We started humming the tune, much to the anger of our guards.

The rest of the police returned after just a few minutes. They uncuffed us and told us to leave the area. As we didn't have tickets for the game, they warned us not to try to gain admission. We would be instantly re-arrested. They also warned us that we had been walking in the wrong direction and kindly gave us directions to where we could find a tram to take us back to the station.

They left us and we began the walk back to the tram stop, relieved at not having been arrested or deported. We found the stop and the tram duly arrived to take us back into the town. I was still quite nervous and fully expected mobs of Dutch hooligans to be roaming the streets in search of English stragglers.

The streets were very quiet and most of the bars appeared to be shut. This left us with the problem of where to watch the big game. There was only a few of us and we suspected that the majority of English lads were either in the ground, in custody, or on a ferry back to England. When the tram stopped near the train station, we jumped off and found a bar that was open and was showing the football. It was packed with other England fans and we soon recognised faces from the military compound.

We told them all about our daring escape, the ducking and diving each time an enemy car was spotted, and our subsequent recapture by armed police. We felt a little foolish when the other lads explained how they escaped from the compound. When they got off the buses, they had run towards the main gates. The gates weren't locked and the handful of soldiers on guard were not prepared to stop them leaving. They casually walked out of the compound, jumped on a bus into town, and had been sat in here relaxing over a cold beer while we had been risked heart failure.

We watched England battle bravely, but still lose to the Dutch by two goals to nil, effectively ending our chances of qualifying for the 1994 World Cup. A train was leaving Rotterdam just after the game finished, so we decided to catch that train, before the bulk of the Dutch fans had time to make it back from the stadium. The train was packed with England fans and when we arrived back in Amsterdam about an hour later we all went off in search of some much needed beer. We were sat drinking and chatting in a bar when the all too familiar sound of it kicking off could be heard once again out on the streets. We took a quick look to see the usual scene. England fans were involved in more running battles with the Dutch police.

I had seen enough over the last few days and although it had been good fun, the excitement soon wears off. When you are constantly involved in clashes with the police it becomes tedious. You are never going to win and most of the time is spent being chased by coppers who want to beat you and then imprison you. Throwing bottles and running has never excited me in the same way that it excites Rangers and Celtic fans. Sticking up for yourselves against foreigners who want to take a pop at you is fine, but fighting the police just for the sake of it doesn't interest me. Later, I did hear that Ajax fans were involved in some of the clashes with England fans when they returned to Amsterdam, but I never saw any of that. I had already returned to my hotel where I met some of the Australian girls who were also staying there. They had been out on the town earlier on that evening, but became concerned at the rowdy behaviour of the English fans and so had returned to the hotel to enjoy a quiet drink and a smoke.

I was having a drink with these girls when a few more of their mates came into the bar. 'Fucking hell,' they exclaimed. 'Those Pommie soccer players are still fighting out there.'

I laughed at the thought of David Platt and Tony Adams rampaging through the red light district. Although to be fair, someone like Adams would probably have jumped at the chance.

Dublin, 1995

ENGLAND'S FAILURE TO qualify for the 1994 World Cup led to the departure of Graham Taylor and his successor was Cockney wide boy and loveable rogue, Terry Venables. His appointment lifted the gloom for England fans and his first game in charge was a friendly at home to Denmark. A sell out crowd generated a wonderful atmosphere, and optimism was high that El Tel would turn out to be the messiah English football so desperately needed after the frustration of Taylor's reign.

Our failure to qualify for the World Cup and the fact that we were hosting the 1996 European Championships meant that we had no competitive fixtures to play for three long years. In their wisdom, the FA arranged to play Ireland in a friendly at Lansdowne Road in February 1995 to compensate.

By now I had become disillusioned with following England away from home. The constant aggravation was no longer enjoyable and I preferred to spend my time and money on less dangerous pastimes. I still took a keen interest in England and the behaviour of the fans, but when the Irish fixture was announced, I had no intention of making the trip. I had already been to Dublin and although it was exciting at the time, I was relieved to have got out of there without being arrested or hurt. I had also grown up a little bit since 1990 and could not be bothered with all the running back and forth. My opinion at the time was that you were deliberately putting yourself in a very dangerous position and for what? A bit of excitement and, all things going well, a good laugh down the pub with your mates when you got home and told your stories. However, it was not guaranteed that all things would go well and I didn't want to run the risk of facing up to the repercussions of getting arrested or deported.

A few weeks before the big game that I wasn't going to go to, I was sat in my local on a Sunday lunchtime, drinking and talking about football. The subject of the Ireland game was brought up and the topic of conversation naturally centred around whether or not we should make the trip. I can't remember exactly what was said, but the following day I found myself in the travel agents, booking three flights to Dublin for the day before the match.

The big day soon arrived and we arrived at Gatwick early in the morning to catch our flight to Dublin. There were hardly any other English fans on the aeroplane and the flight passed relatively smoothly, apart from the terrible turbulence experienced over the Irish sea.

Dublin itself was fairly familiar to me from my last visit to the fair city five years earlier. We jumped on a bus to the city centre and this time headed straight to the tourist information office in O'Connell Street. A friendly young Irish girl found us a hotel just out of the centre of the town that was within our price range. We took the directions and walked up O'Connell Street towards our home for the duration of our visit.

Shortly after leaving the city centre we entered a very unpleasant looking area. Our hotel was right in the heart of this estate and although it didn't look too dangerous in the light, I wasn't looking forward to walking back there at night.

We dumped our bags, had a shower and went for a drink in the local pub. Surprisingly enough, the pub was done out fairly nicely and wasn't full of the expected drug addicts or even English hating Provos. All of the customers were old men sitting quietly, staring into their whiskey or watching the racing on the television. We got chatting to the landlord, who was friendly enough, and to a couple of the old boys at the bar. It wasn't the most happening bar I have ever frequented, but it would do for a few beers and a chat.

After a while we ordered some lunch. I fancied an Irish stew, but as I had never had it before, I opted for just a small bowl for 50 pence. A huge bowl duly arrived and was feverishly eaten, washed down by yet another pint of Harp. My mate decided he would also have a bowl and went for the large bowl which was double the money at a pound. When it arrived a few minutes later, it was the same size, if not smaller, than the small bowl! The Irish are a friendly people, but they do have some strange quirks to their nature.

After a couple of hours in this pub, we left and walked down O'Connell Street. A few pubs had bouncers on the doors and were refusing to let large groups of English fans in. The pubs without bouncers were all busy with England fans and were doing a roaring trade.

We did a bit of a crawl round the pubs to see if any of the boys who we knew had come over. Chelsea were playing away in Bruges the following week, and I knew that a lot of their boys had chosen to give this trip a miss so that they could afford the trip to Belgium.

Most of the pubs had small groups of Northerners sitting around chatting amongst themselves. Generally speaking, the England fans were a lot younger than you normally see away. It might just have been me getting older, but they all seemed to be in their late teens. They were all under the impression that every Irish person they met was an IRA terrorist or sympathiser, and as such they were rude and obnoxious to their hosts.

In many ways, I could understand their anger as I had a similar attitude when I was nineteen. Having said that, I wasn't rude to every person I met in the same way as these fans were. One particular pub was full with lads from Burnley and Shrewsbury. The Shrewsbury lads came over as soon as we walked in. 'What firm are you?' they demanded to know.

'Do we look like a firm? I asked. After all, there was only three of us. I explained that two of us were Millwall fans and the other lad was a West Ham fan.

This confused the wannabe hooligan. 'But you lot hate each other,' he observed.

We explained that, yes, generally speaking Millwall and West Ham supporters do hate each other, but as we come from the same town and drink in the same pubs, we were in fact friends. We tried to walk away from this clueless clown, but he joined us at the bar.

'Hoy, you Irish slut, give us some more lager, and none of that Irish piss.' This was his way of ordering a drink, and although the pretty Irish girl served him, the look of disgust in her eyes was clear for all to see.

I was embarrassed to be stood next to this idiot in case the girl thought we were friends. I also felt sorry for her having to put up with such vile abuse from a bunch of immature idiots. We politely ordered our drinks and tried to avoid contact with the Shrewsbury lads.

Millwall had been in the news that week as there had been trouble at our Cup game with Chelsea. The Shrewsbury lad asked if I was there and wanted to know all about it. 'Yeah, I was there, but nothing much happened.' This was not entirely true, but I just didn't want to get involved in a conversation with this half-wit and his stupid mates. Eventually, they got the message and returned to their seats.

Just as I thought I might enjoy a quiet drink with my mates, we were approached by yet another pissed up half-wit, this time from Burnley. 'Where's the rest of your boys?' he asked.

'Look mate, there's three of us here, no more, no less,' I replied.

'Yeah, but Millwall and West Ham have got hundreds of boys between them. They must have a firm here.'

He failed to comprehend the idea that three lads could travel on their own to a game without the need to be travelling as part of a mob from one particular team. I asked him if this was his first England away game, although I knew what the answer would be. It was pretty clear from his behaviour that he had probably never set foot out of Burnley in his life.

He confirmed that it was his first time away with England and then proceeded to tell me all about the exploits of the Burnley Suicide Squad. Now, I know enough to realise that Burnley do indeed have a good mob and that it can be a very dangerous place to visit. I've even met a few of their boys on previous trips and have nothing but respect for them. However, from the way he was talking, Burnley was the only violent city in the country, their mob had travelled all over the country taking liberties in every town they visited, and him and his mates were their top boys.

I soon got bored with his never ending stories of how tough they all were. Another Burnley fan interrupted and asked if we wanted to buy any drugs. We had now finished our drinks, so we made our excuses and left. It was obvious the Burnley and Shrewsbury lads didn't like us much, but the feeling was mutual. There was no doubt they would have liked to have had a go at us, but as there was only three of us, even they realised it would have been pointless. As it turned out, I later heard they ended up fighting each other that night, probably when they could no longer take any more drink.

We carried on going from pub to pub, and generally speaking, all the England fans we met were from the north. They were a lot younger than the fans you normally saw at away games and Southerners were conspicuous by their absence. I've got nothing against Northerners and have met many decent, staunch and patriotic Northerners on my travels. The fact is though that both Northerners and Southerners prefer to stick with their own kind.

In the past, there has been trouble between Southerners and Northerners at away games, but fortunately I have never witnessed it at first hand. It is something I strongly disagree with as we are all English and should stick together on our travels. I have often drunk with many lads from different teams throughout the north, and on occasions have been grateful to them for backing us up when trouble has kicked off.

The atmosphere on this trip was like no other I had experienced before. The Irish people are incredibly friendly, but like any big city, Dublin has its fair share of gangs. At no point though did I see any gangs of Irish hooligans on the look out for English. There wasn't even a heavy police presence in the town. With no one to fight with, the English soon got bored and violent arguments between rival fans soon developed into full scale fights. There wasn't any of the usual banter you get from other fans. It was simply a question of who are you, how many of you are here, and if you were from London, then it wasn't very pleasant.

We were on our way into one pub when five or six lads came out. We got chatting to them and it turned out they were from Luton. Some were Luton Town fans, others were Spurs, and one of the Spurs fans was bleeding from a busted nose. They told us that a mob of Leeds fans had just gone into the pub and started playing up because these lads were from the South. They warned the three of us to keep out of that pub.

We took their advice and soon found another pub. This pub was packed with Leicester City fans. Although they were all fairly well dressed, they looked pathetic as every one of them was dressed head to toe in Ralph Lauren gear. It is quite nice gear and at that time it was quite fashionable, but this mob was overdoing it slightly.

We stood at the bar where we got chatting to a Chelsea fan from Beckenham. Like most Chelsea fans, he didn't care much for Leicester fans so he was pleased to see a few Southerners in the bar with him. He was clued up and knew the Chelsea scene very well.

We were enjoying his company when a couple of lads came towards us. They had spotted that we were Southerners, as everyone who goes to football knows that you can always tell a Northerner and a Southerner apart, just by looking at them. They came over and told us they were West Ham fans. This didn't impress me much, but to be fair, they were immaculately dressed, sober, and looked very capable. They asked us if the bar was accepting English currency. When we told them that the bar had been taking our English money, they quickly ordered two drinks and paid for them with brand new crisp £50 notes. They took their change, gulped down their drinks and left the bar, giving us a knowing smile as they left.

The Leicester boys were getting louder and louder and generally winding up our new found mate from Chelsea. I wonder if the Leicester boys would have been so wide if the usual Chelsea faces were there instead of in Bruges. It certainly seemed to me that the different mobs of Northerners were determined to stamp their mark and demonstrate that they were the top mob at England games now. I'm not a big fan of Chelsea, and I hate to admit it, but to be honest, they had the top boys at England games throughout the Eighties and Nineties. Watching these idiots, raring up at each other and generally just being childish, made me come over a little sentimental. If the Chelsea boys had been there, they would not have allowed it to go on.

On our way to yet another pub, we saw more clashes between rival fans. It was getting beyond a joke and I was starting to get annoyed. I hadn't come over to Dublin to fight with Northerners. If that was what I wanted, I could have got that most Saturdays in the league games. I had come over to Dublin to have a drink, chat to fellow Englishmen, and if the Irish wanted to fight, then fair play. As it was clear there wasn't going to be any problems with the Irish, there was no reason for there to be any trouble at all. We decided to return to the pub up near our hotel and let the Northerners get on with what it was they wanted to do.

When we arrived back in our favourite pub, the atmosphere was completely different to that seen in other parts of the town. The pub was busy and, as at lunch time, the clientele consisted primarily of old men, drinking Guinness and whiskey. The landlord soon got chatting to us again and was well aware of the trouble going on in O'Connell Street and the surrounding areas. 'Why can't the English have a drink and just enjoy the crack?' he asked.

It was a reasonable question that had been asked hundreds of times before. I was usually capable of answering it by sticking up for my fellow England fans. The usual reasons would be given such as police brutality or rival fans provoking them, but on this occasion, I could offer no reasonable explanation beyond the fact that the fans had got drunk and had just wanted to fight. It was as simple as that. If the Irish people or the Irish police didn't want to be a part of it, then fine, they will just fight each other.

The people in this pub were incredibly friendly and treated us like lords. They seemed genuinely pleased that we had gone slightly out of town to find a genuine Irish pub. The landlord explained that the following day, the big game was being shown live on a large screen television in the pub. As we didn't have tickets for the game he said we were welcome to watch it in his pub. It was a kind offer and after the unruly behaviour of the majority of England fans, it was a little surprising that the Irish people were still offering the hand of friendship to any English football fans.

By closing time, we were all well pissed and now had to face the dodgy walk back to the hotel. It was only a five minute walk, but everyone in the pub had warned us to be careful. It was a dangerous area at the best of times, but with so many England fans causing problems in the town, it was highly likely that a few local boys would be hanging around, looking to pick off stray England fans. The amount of alcohol we had consumed helped to erase our fears and we strutted out of the pub and down to the local fish and chip shop. There were a few young Irish tearaways, aged about twelve or thirteen, hanging around. They clocked we were English straight away and at first started to give us a bit of stick. When they saw how drunk we were though, they just started laughing at us and telling us how we were going to get thrashed the following day.

On the day of the game, we woke up in time for opening time and went back down to our local pub. The weather was constantly changing, with hail stones, thunder storms, and gusting winds, all in the space of a few minutes. The warmth of the pub and its open fire and cold beer was like a breath of fresh air. We had planned to stay in here just for one beer before going off in search of tickets for the game, but as it turned out, we stayed in there for a few hours. Every time we got up to leave, we took one look at the weather and ordered another beer.

Eventually we did leave and walked down to O'Connell Street. A lot of the England fans were still in the area. They were a lot quieter than the previous night, but just as aggressive. There was still no friendly banter, just evil stares and menacing looks. I was cold, ticketless and hungry and really didn't fancy watching a football match with these fans. It was obvious they were going to kick it off big time and I really didn't want to be part of it.

We came across a couple of touts, but tickets were not going cheap so we decided to return to our safe, friendly and warm pub and watch the match on the big screen. It was still a few hours to go to kick-off and the pub was fairly quiet. We continued drinking all afternoon as the pub became busier by the minute. By kick-off time, the pub was packed and we were the only three England fans in the place. Everyone knew we were English and they were giving us plenty of stick. A couple of lads who were sat at the bar clearly didn't like us being there, but we weren't going to let these idiots ruin our night and we just ignored them.

The drinkers in the pub went crazy when Ireland took the lead early in the game. I was disappointed that we were one goal down, but I had to laugh because of the amount of piss-taking we were getting from the Irish. A few minutes later, England equalised and the three of us went mad, shouting and laughing at everyone in the pub. Our moment of glory was short lived as the goal was disallowed, much to the delight of everyone else in the pub, and to our absolute horror.

After the goal had been disallowed, the television cameras focused on the England fans in the upper tier of the stand. They were fighting in the stand, ripping up seats and throwing them either on to the pitch or at the fans in the lower tiers. The police didn't appear to have a clue as to what to do to contain the trouble and their failure to respond just meant that the English could continue to cause trouble. The trouble soon escalated, and fans desperate to escape the danger were forced to run on to the pitch. The referee had no alternative but to abandon the game. I watched these events unfold live on television in a pub packed with Irish football fans. At that moment, they must have hated the English football fans, and yet they were still as good as gold to the three of us.

They kept on asking us why the fans were causing trouble. None of the Irish fans wanted trouble - in fact, most left the ground as soon as the trouble started. They just couldn't understand why the English were causing so much trouble. I couldn't offer a reasonable explanation either, but continued to watch the events on the television. It seemed to me that fans in the upper tier were throwing seats and other missiles on to other England fans in the seats in the lower tier.

Obviously, I wasn't at the ground so I don't know for sure what may have sparked the trouble. However, I was in the town the previous night and at lunchtime before the game, and it was clear that a lot of the England fans were hell bent on fighting each other. Perhaps a dispute between two rival mobs had escalated into the carnage we were now witnessing.

The popular theory at the time was that it was organised by Combat 18, a neo-Nazi organisation strongly opposed to the IRA. At the time, the British Government was just beginning their sell out to the IRA, and many English fans were genuinely angry at the way the

Government was surrendering to murderers. The majority of English fans who travel away do harbour nationalist beliefs and there is no doubt that most of them would have been disgusted with the Government and may have chosen this fixture as the ideal platform to vent their anger and show their disgust. However, there were a few thousand fans over in Dublin and only a handful of those would have had any serious links with Combat 18. I think it is pushing it a little too far to suggest that all the trouble was orchestrated by one particular organisation.

The English fans have demonstrated in the past that they are perfectly capable of causing large scale disorder without any leadership, as events in Luxembourg, Turin and Basle clearly demonstrated. In Dublin, on the Tuesday night and at Lansdowne Road, the Irish police were completely overwhelmed by the sheer numbers of England fans that were up for causing trouble. They should have known what the English fans would get up to if they were poorly policed.

The trouble in Dublin in 1990 was far worse than anything that went down on this occasion, and on top of that the English police had warned the Dublin authorities that hundreds, if not thousands, of well known and notorious hooligans were coming over to Dublin without tickets for the game. Their failure to act on this information led to the scenes in the ground that were witnessed all over the world and caused great embarrassment to the British Government.

At the end of the day, the English fans were ultimately responsible for the trouble. There is no disputing that and no point in trying to deny it. The fact is that most of them will be proud of what went on over there and will have viewed the trip as a success. They had a good ruck, a good laugh, and made a point of showing the Government that they shouldn't have surrendered to the IRA.

There is no point in blaming the fans. They won't be embarrassed, and they certainly won't stop travelling to games just because they are widely condemned in the media. People should aim their frustrations at the authorities who were responsible for preventing the trouble that so many fans enjoy indulging in. Where were the police on Tuesday night and Wednesday afternoon? Why had they let fans into the ground without tickets? Why wasn't their adequate segregation in the ground? Why did the Irish authorities fail to heed the advice of the English police? Why was the game played at such a politically sensitive time? These are the questions that need to be answered if the authorities want to ensure that there is no trouble at future games between Ireland and England.

It is all too easy to blame the fans, but that doesn't tell the full story of Dublin. The fact is that there will always be fans who want to cause trouble. The authorities know that and it is their job to prevent these fans from having the opportunity to cause mayhem. If they fail in their duties, they should hold their hands up and take at least some of the blame.

I spent the rest of the evening drinking in the pub, and apart from the couple of idiots at the bar, the Irish behaved well towards us, despite having ample reason to hate us for being English.

The following day, we returned to the pub before catching our flight home. We had another drink with the landlord and expressed our gratitude for his hospitality. Once again, the two lads who didn't like us were at the bar, and this time one of them muttered something under his breath as we walked past. Before we had an opportunity to say anything back, the landlord stepped in and told the two lads to piss off.

Once back at the airport, we checked in for our flight and went for a drink in the airport bar. Our mate from Chelsea was there and we got chatting to him once again. We had only been stood at the bar a few seconds when my mate noticed one of the other England fans staring at him. After a few seconds, the lad came over and went straight up to my mate. 'Are you a Brummie?' he asked in a very threatening manner.

As soon as my mate replied, it was clear he didn't have a Birmingham accent and the other lad relaxed a little. He explained that he was a Notts Forest fan and had a personal grudge with a Birmingham fan because the blue nose had sold some photographs to a newspaper. The photographs were from a fight at a previous England game and clearly showed the Forest boy getting stuck in. The photographs had been seen by his boss and had cost him his job. The Forest boy apologised for the case of mistaken identity and we soon got chatting to him. He was a big lad and looked a right handful, but he was a decent lad and knew his stuff.

Looking back on it, it was a strange trip in many ways. I had enjoyed it, and didn't regret going at all, but this was mainly down to the friendliness of the Irish, when really they had every reason to resent us being there. You normally meet so many decent lads on England trips, but on this occasion, we only met the lads from Chelsea and Forest who were friendly, knowledgeable and good company. It was enough to put me off going to future away games. I didn't want to be part of a mob that had no standards and I didn't want to risk fighting with other English fans simply because of the fact that I was from the South East. I was also getting a bit older and wiser and didn't want to spend hundreds of pounds on socialising with eighteen year olds who were desperate to look hard and make a name for themselves.

I personally didn't think the trouble was as bad as the media portrayed. The reason the condemnation was so widespread was because the trouble took place inside the ground, in full view of millions of people watching the game live on television. Basically, the trouble was between rival firms of England fans, primarily from the North, and involved throwing missiles or fighting with the police.

If the trouble had erupted inside Anfield or Highbury, for example, the police would have contained the situation within seconds. This type of behaviour goes on at nearly every England away game and also happens quite often at League games in this country. Since the large stadiums in this country and most other Western European nations are usually quite secure and well policed, the trouble invariably takes place away from the ground. As such, a lot of people do not see exactly what goes on and the trouble goes largely unreported by the media.

The English media reported on the events in their usual hysterical manner. The far right organisations took the brunt of the blame and all the fans were labelled as mindless morons. The press managed to persuade an alleged Millwall fan from Milton Keynes to offer his opinions on the trouble. Why a Millwall fan? There was only a handful of Millwall fans there. Why didn't they ask Stoke, Birmingham or Carlisle fans for their stories? They were the most active firms over there, but again, the press just aren't interested in establishing the facts. Hooliganism equals thugs. Thugs equals Millwall. So let's get a Millwall fan to speak about it. The bloke they got hold off has never been seen at any of the Millwall games I have been to, and Milton Keynes is hardly regarded as a staunch Millwall area. He was probably just someone who was gullible enough to give the media what they wanted.

The usual questions were asked about why fans behave in this fashion. We have all heard the reasons offered by the experts, but in my opinion they always miss the most obvious answer. To many people it is simply fun and exciting to indulge in this type of behaviour. The questions they should be asking are why the police continually fail to prevent trouble kicking off despite having the resources and know how to deal with the problems as and when they happen. These are the important issues that need to be addressed if the authorities are seriously trying to eradicate the problem. The press, as always, take the easy option and just slag off the fans without offering any solutions to the "hooligan menace". Still, if they came up with some answers, what would they fill their pages with?

Euro 96

THE EUROPEAN FOOTBALL Championship was taking place in the summer of 1996 in England and it was the first major international football tournament to be staged in England since the World Cup 30 years earlier. As everyone knows, we won the World Cup in 1966 and the nation was confident that we could repeat that success this time around.

The Football Association had been planning the tournament for some time and as expected decided to extract every last penny from football fans throughout Europe who planned to holiday in England to watch the games. The cities hosting the matches also grew wise to the potential revenue that could be made, hence the increased hotel prices and similar ways of getting extra money from the fans.

The FA had also fixed it so that if England won their group, they would play each one of their matches at the 'venue of legends', otherwise known as Wembley. From their point of view, I suppose this would generate more money since Wembley was by far the largest of the stadiums being used. However, I felt this decision was unfair and I was surprised UEFA allowed the English FA to go ahead with this plan as it potentially could have given England an unfair advantage.

I also felt it was unfair from a supporter's point of view. I personally do not like Wembley and feel England should play at other grounds throughout the country, saving Wembley for just the major show piece international matches. The atmosphere at some of the smaller venues would be a lot more intimidating than the family atmosphere experienced at Wembley. Fans throughout the country would also have a chance to watch England play without the hassle of getting to and from Wembley. I live in the South East, but would rather make a day of it and travel to Villa Park or Old Trafford to watch England play than spend hours getting to Wembley only to be ripped off by the FA when you eventually get there.

From a security point of view there was no doubt that England offered the safest place in the whole of Europe to stage a major football tournament. There are a number of reasons for this. Now, I am no fan of the English police, but I have to give them my grudging respect when you compare them to the police in every other European country. By and large, they weigh up each situation and usually prevent trouble starting, whereas foreign police tend to just wait for the inevitable outbreak of trouble before steaming in and randomly striking out and arresting anyone in the area. They don't really care who they arrest or hit, but experience tells me that it is usually the English that get caught whether or not they are the aggressors or the victims. This is not to say that the English police don't also strike out at random on occasion, but they are not in the same league as the Dutch, Italian or Spanish police forces, no way.

The English police also use intelligence, not a word that I would normally associate with the Old Bill. In the build up to the tournament, they made many high profile arrests following clashes at games in the domestic leagues. Fans from Arsenal, Tottenham and Newcastle, amongst others, were arrested in high profile dawn raids. These raids were accompanied by television crews and were then broadcast on the national news programmes, presumably as a deterrent to other potential hooligans. The message was clear. The police were ready and waiting for any hooligans who were hoping to cause trouble in England, be they from England or from abroad. From a legal perspective though, the police didn't appear to care that this extensive television coverage may prejudice the fairness of the trials the arrested fans might expect to receive.

Security in and around the top grounds in England is amongst the best in the world with effective segregation, closed circuit television, and the well rehearsed procedures developed by the police through bitter years of bitter experience dealing with crowd disorder. The police knew the main boys from each club that might cause trouble and those fans also knew the police. This wasn't going to stop these boys from doing what they felt they had to do, but it certainly gave the police the advantage.

However, the main reason why there would be less trouble by staging a tournament in England, rather than say Germany or France, was simply down to the bottle of the hooligans from the competing nations. Or, more to the point, the lack of it. The English media were having a field day with their ridiculous claims that fans from Holland, Italy, Spain, and Germany were coming over to show the English that they were now the top dogs in Europe. The English may have started exporting violence abroad, but these foreigners were coming over to show the English that their days were over. I don't know whether the media invented all of these stories or not, or whether some hard nuts from Rotterdam, Cologne and Rome did actually say these things. Either way, they were making the English fans laugh. We all knew that these foreign firms never turn up in England. Quite often, they do not even turn up at their home games, let alone coming over and taking it to the English in their own back yard. The Germans apparently went as far as saying they were going to do what Hitler failed to do during the war. As we say down at Millwall, let 'em come.

In all honesty, most of these claims were probably completely fabricated by the press. They like to stir up trouble and then act holier than thou when their predictions bear fruit. They should know by now that irresponsible reporting like this can do no good at all and they should hold their hands up and accept a share of the blame. Out of all the threats being reported in the papers though, one set of fans was particularly conspicuous by their absence.

Scotland had qualified for the tournament and as such would be playing three matches in England. No more than this though, because that would have meant qualifying for the later stages of a tournament, a feat that appears to be beyond them. The press like to portray the travelling Scotsman as a loveable rogue - loud, brash, pissed up, but incredibly friendly. To be fair, the majority of them are like this when they travel abroad. If they want to wear skirts and befriend Germans, fair play to them. It's not the way I would chose to behave, but fortunately I was born south of the wall. However, when the Scots come to England, their national characteristics change. The majority of them still wear skirts, but in addition to their strange sense of style, they also carry a chip on each shoulder. They certainly do not want to befriend the English and prefer to sing about some silly war that took place way back in 1314.

The Scots had not played in England since 1988 when the game was marred by serious crowd trouble. The last time they played England was in 1989 and that game had also seen serious crowd trouble. Without doubt, both sides had a few scores to settle with each other. Many England and Scotland boys get on with each other and keep in regular touch. A few teams even have alliances with each other such as Hearts and Portsmouth, Rangers and Chelsea, Aberdeen and Tottenham, Oldham and Hibs, and Dundee and Stoke. Some of these alliances may not be as strong as they were, but the fact is the English and Scottish fans can communicate with each other without resorting to making idle threats via the newspapers. And although the papers didn't seem to be aware of it, the English and Scottish firms were making plans to meet each other.

When the draw was made for the opening stages of the tournament, England was paired with Switzerland, Scotland and Holland in that order. Unfortunately, the England games had already been sold out before the draw had been made and corporate bodies had snapped up most of the tickets. I didn't stand a chance of obtaining a ticket through the official channels and wasn't prepared to pay the prices quoted by the touts in London. In any case, there was only one game that really interested me, the battle with Scotland

As England had qualified automatically for the tournament, they had only played friendly internationals since 1994. Their form in the build up to the tournament had not been great, and Alan Shearer was in the middle of a barren run of not scoring. The press were getting on the team's backs and suggesting that Shearer should be dropped from the team.

Matters came to a head during a pre-tournament friendly in Hong Kong. The players had been allowed to go out on the town after the game to celebrate Paul Gascoigne's birthday. These lads are young, fit men, and quite reasonably, their night out would centre around getting pissed up. Photographs soon surfaced in the papers showing certain players stretched out in a dentist chair while the barmen squirted shots of alcohol in their mouths. If this was not bad enough, there were also reports that trouble had erupted on the Cathay Pacific flight back home.

The players were a bit naive if they felt they could get away with this behaviour without the press going over the top, but surely that is all they could be found guilty of. I am not condemning them for their behaviour because it was obviously just high jinks amongst friends that may have got a little out of hand. What was totally out of order was the sensational coverage given to these alleged incidents by the tabloid press. There were hysterical calls for the players to be named and shamed and withdrawn from the squad. Paul Gascoigne was named as the chief culprit without any evidence apart from the fact that it happened to be his birthday.

It was scandalous reporting, but in hindsight, may have worked in our favour. The players felt they had been unfairly picked on and maintained a collective vow of silence. It created a them and us situation and the squad was clearly determined to ram the words right back up the arses of the journalists who were so quick to condemn them. The laughable thing is that most of these journalists behave in the same fashion when they travel abroad to report on England games.

The tournament opened with England playing Switzerland at Wembley. Things started very well and even the opening ceremony was not as bad as I feared it would be. One of the highlights was St George on a horse slaying the dragon. This was a very nationalistic symbol and it was good to see that our heritage could be displayed without the usual cries of racism. I half expected there to be demands that St George should also carry the flag of the European Union so as not to offend any Europeans in the crowd. Well, sod them. This is England and the English people should be proud of our illustrious history.

Alan Shearer opened the scoring early in the first half, but Switzerland slowly got back into the game and eventually scored a deserved equaliser. Over all, the performance and the final result was a little disappointing. Like so many other England fans who regularly attend football matches in this country, I had watched the game in my local pub. It was a shame to be with so many people who would have loved to have been at Wembley that afternoon, but who couldn't get a ticket for love nor money.

Wembley appeared to be full of people you normally meet in the supermarket rather than on the terraces. They had hijacked the occasion, and although they managed to create a lively atmosphere, it was nothing compared to what might have happened if the genuine fans had obtained tickets.

The following week, Scotland were coming to London, along with the famous Tartan Army for the first time in eight years. Although I didn't have a ticket for the game, I had come up with an idea on how I could get one. A work colleague was a devoted Liverpool fan, but despite holding a season ticket, he had failed to secure a ticket for the FA Cup Final against their arch-rivals, Manchester United. However, he was lucky enough to be in possession of two tickets for the Scotland match. He made it clear that he would be happy to swap the two Scotland tickets for one FA Cup Final ticket.

The Football Association has a ridiculous method of distributing tickets for the FA Cup Final. Only a limited number of tickets go on sale at the clubs involved in the match. A sizeable chunk of tickets is distributed evenly to every club affiliated to the FA and so a Sunday league player from say Wiltshire has more chance of securing a ticket than a Liverpool fan from Bootle. Rather than go to the game, the Sunday league player will normally sell the ticket to a tout for a huge bundle of notes and leave the Scouser with no alternative but to mug the tout outside Wembley.

As it happened, I knew a footballer that had a Cup Final ticket for sale. I managed to persuade the two parties to swap the tickets, which meant that the footballer now had two Scotland tickets for sale. I seized my opportunity and paid £150 for both of them. The footballer had £150, the Liverpool fan had his Cup ticket and I had two tickets for the Scotland game. Everyone was happy.

The tabloid press was fairly quiet in the week building up to the big game. The goal by Shearer had silenced his critics and the possibility of trouble at the Scotland game was hardly mentioned. However, things started to liven up on Thursday night when a large mob of Aberdeen casuals started turning up in London. Trouble erupted in the pubs around Camden that night in a foretaste of what was surely to come.

Friday night saw the arrival of many more Scots. These were the usual types of Scots who headed to Trafalgar Square to sing and be merry. They entertained the tourists by singing their silly songs and showing their hairy arses, whilst chanting anti-England songs. Not surprisingly, there were a number of clashes in the West End that night between small groups of rival fans.

Come Saturday morning, I was up early and in London before opening time. I had decided to avoid the potential flash points at Trafalgar Square and Baker Street and headed instead for Hampstead. There are a few nice pubs in that area and once you have finished drinking, it's only a short ride on the tube to Wembley.

Most of the England fans heading to the game were clad in brand new England shirts and draped in St George flags. Many had their faces painted too. Similarly, the Scots were dressed in tartan, ginger wigs and their faces were painted with the flag of St Andrew. And by and large, both sets of fans were getting on with each other. The Scots were loud and chanting about the battle of Bannockburn, and this appeared to amuse most of the England fans who clearly didn't understand the significance of this battle.

I kept a close eye on the behaviour of these fans and couldn't believe how gullible most of the England fans were. The Scots were clearly baiting the English, but most of them were too thick to realise the historical meaning of the songs. These England fans had probably never been to an England game before and it was a disgrace that the genuine fans who had been unable to obtain tickets were not here to stand up to the Scots.

What upset me most was the fact that there were thousands of lads sat in their local pubs in Stockport, Stoke, Brighton, or wherever, who would have given their right arm to be in London, facing up to the Scots. While they were hundreds of miles away nursing their beers, I had to witness the England fans being laughed at by the Scots.

I could and maybe should have gone into the West End to meet up with the casuals from all over the country who had converged on London to take on the Scots. However, times had changed and I was getting older. I couldn't be bothered to get involved in the clashes any more. As I was lucky enough to have a ticket, I just wanted to have a drink and watch the game. We soon found a pub in Hampstead and fortunately got chatting to some lads from Luton who did know a thing or two about football. There were a few Scots in the pub, but generally the mood in the pub was light hearted.

Before we knew it, it was time to head to Wembley and be surrounded by yet more part-time England fans. Unlike previous matches between the two nations, this time the Scots had not over run Wembley. However, despite being heavily out numbered, they were still chanting their songs without any retaliation from the England fans. We did bump into a small group of England casuals, but as they were from West Ham I didn't really want to stick with them. In any event, I didn't want to get into any trouble and be arrested before the game.

Inside the stadium we found our seats and were amazed to find ourselves surrounded by hordes of Japanese tourists, eagerly taking photographs of anything that moved. The Scots were behind the goal to our left and were creating a wonderful atmosphere. Whilst they were singing about Bannockburn and Jimmy Hill, the England fans were continually chanting 'Football's coming home!'

Call me a spoilsport if you like, but I think *Three Lions* is the most annoying football song ever written. It was adopted as some kind of anthem by plastic football fans who had suddenly discovered football and had now hijacked the game from the true fans. Girls in pubs were singing this song as if it actually meant something to them. Thirty years of hurt? How could these people possibly relate to that line when they had only discovered football when the Premier League was formed just a few years earlier? And these people had only become interested in the national team when they had become lucky enough to obtain tickets for these matches. Where were these people in the Eighties when the FA struggled to pull in 20,000 fans for many of the games held at Wembley?

As a true football fan, you can't really appreciate the good times unless you have experienced the bad times. Therefore, the meaning behind that line would have no significance to the majority of fans that attended any of the England games in Euro '96. The people who had experienced years of hurt, mismanagement, lies, and let downs, were stuck in the pubs in their home towns because, once again, the FA had sold out to the new breed of fans and the corporate bodies.

The Scottish anthem was played, and we naturally booed and whistled loudly throughout. People around us looked at us in disgust. When the English anthem was played, we belted it out with all our heart. Again, people looked at us in disgust. Well, fuck them! It appears that it is now a crime at England games to be patriotic and to intimidate the opposition. It's okay for the Scots to sing about killing the English and to boo our anthem, but if we behave in a similar fashion we're viewed as the bad guys. These plastic English fans obviously believed the hype about what wonderful supporters the Scots were. They wouldn't have been so naive if they had seen what I had seen over the years.

As far as the game itself was concerned, it truly was a memorable encounter. Scotland had the better of the first half, but failed to take their chances. The score at half-time was 0-0, but the Scots were confident they would go on to win. Throughout the half-time break, they were singing and dancing and genuinely appeared to believe they were on their way to victory.

The second half was a different story though and early on Shearer headed England into the lead. The Scots fought back and were eventually awarded a penalty and the ideal opportunity to get themselves back into the game. The Scots went crazy, but their delight was short lived. Just as McAllister was about to strike the ball past a helpless David Seaman, a sudden change of wind direction caused the ball to move slightly, causing the Scottish captain to miss hit the ball (a poor excuse if ever I heard one). The penalty was saved and the England fans went crazy for the second time in the game.

The Scots were down hearted and as they argued about the wind direction, Paul Gascoigne was busy making a fool out of his

Rangers team mate, Colin Hendry, sending him first one way and then the other before chipping the ball over his head and volleying the ball past a helpless Jim Leighton. It was a wonderful goal and was celebrated in wonderful fashion by England fans and players alike. Gazza lay down behind the goal while McManaman and others squirted water into his mouth in a mock reconstruction of the events in Hong Kong. While I was still celebrating, the Scottish fans were in tears behind the goal, a sight that made me even happier. My only negative thought at the time was for the people that couldn't be with me. Instead of being surrounded by clueless Japanese tourists and part-time glory hunting England fans, I would have preferred to have been in the company of genuine supporters. Unfortunately, it was not to be.

We beat the Jocks 2-0 and I was over the moon. However, directly outside Wembley, the atmosphere was muted. The Scots were distraught and we were giving them plenty of stick as they began their long journey home. Most England fans were behaving as if they had just left the theatre after watching a satisfactory production. They quietly made their way home, pleased that the players had kept them entertained for 90 minutes. To them that is what football is all about.

There are many ways to be entertained, but being a football fan, the last thing on your mind is entertainment. There is a terrace culture in England that is rapidly dying out, but the sad thing is that most of these people were not even aware it existed in the first place. The cult of the football casual is dying out, of that there is no doubt, and the events in and around Wembley proved to me that football is changing beyond recognition.

The casual will never die out completely though, despite the best efforts of the authorities. While the players were fighting it out on the hallowed turf of Wembley, the English and Scottish casuals were fighting it out in the West End of London. None of the casuals had tickets for the game but, people had come from as far as Carlisle, Plymouth and Aberdeen to participate in the brawl. The English had the numbers, but were mainly in small groups throughout the West End. The Scots had a couple of hundred casuals who chose to stick together. As usual, their boys came mainly from the East Coast of Scotland and consisted of the usual mobs from Aberdeen, Dundee and Edinburgh.

I wasn't in the West End before or after the game and so will not go into the events that took place too deeply for obvious reasons.

However, it has been well documented that the Scots maintained a tight unit and will probably claim a result against the English. There are probably reasons for this, the main one being lack of organisation within the different England mobs. Having said that, this isn't really a reasonable excuse, and I'm sure the Scots could come up with a number of reasons why they took such a pasting in 1989. The Scots earned a lot of respect in London that day, but in my opinion, it was their behaviour before the tournament that struck a chord with me. Unlike the Germans and the Dutch, they didn't bother making threats about what they were going to do. Actions always speak louder than words, and on this occasion, they turned up and did the business. The English casuals didn't forget it, and the opportunity to settle a few scores arose in the double header Battle Of Britain recently.

A few days later, England faced Holland at Wembley in a game that will go down in history as one of the finest performances from an England team ever. The Dutch were cast aside in a show of supreme attacking football which saw England score four times. My own personal highlight was the late consolation goal the Dutch managed to score, because this goal ensured Holland would qualify as runners-up on goal difference ahead of the Scots. The Scots were the ones being sent homeward to think again.

Our next opponents were Spain, and once again I returned to the pub to watch the game. The landlord had agreed to charge £1 a pint until the first goal was scored. Luckily, the game remained goalless for 90 minutes and the game went into extra time. I don't remember much about extra time, but I know it remained goalless as I was still enjoying the cheap lager. England won on penalties and who will ever forget the sight of Stuart Pearce as he scored a crucial penalty and at the same time exorcised the ghosts of Turin six years earlier.

The stage was now set for yet another monumental clash with the Germans in a semi-final of a major tournament. As England were now doing well, the press were fully behind them and therefore had to switch their attention to slagging off the Germans. Unsurprisingly, they went over the top and as they clearly offended many Germans, they were forced to back down and offer their apologies. Obviously, it's okay for the press to offend English players and fans, but not the Germans.

Tickets for the big game had sold out even before the start of the tournament, and unless you had thousands of pounds you stood little chance of getting a ticket. I returned to the same pub which was offering £1 a pint until the first goal was scored, but this time I was unable to take full advantage as Shearer put England ahead in the fourth minute. I didn't care about the beer because suddenly I truly believed we were on our way to beating the Germans in a significant match for the first time in my lifetime.

As always in games between these two nations, it was a fiercely competitive game with both teams giving it their all. The Germans fought their way back into the game and managed to grab an equalising goal. 1-1, and after extra time the two sides were still deadlocked. Once again, a semi-final against Germany would go to penalties. This time, it was Gareth Southgate who was to suffer the devastating consequences of missing the all important shot from 12 yards. Even though Southgate is an ex-Crystal Palace player, and therefore not high in the popularity stakes as far as I am concerned, I would never criticise him for missing the spot kick. It must take an incredible amount of bottle to go up there on your own with the hopes of a nation resting on your ability to hit the ball past the goalkeeper. Southgate will regret missing that penalty for the rest of his life and his disappointment will not be helped by England supporters who continually give him stick about it. Mind you, I'm sure the thousands of pounds he received as a result of laughing about the miss in a TV commercial must have helped to ease the shattering blow.

Once again, there was very little trouble in and around Wembley during or directly after the game. Most of the new plastic football fans at Wembley were probably still too enthralled with the excitement of the evening to have any real understanding of the pain inflicted on the fans who really do care. By now, the Germans had adopted the "Football's Coming Home!" chant as their own, making the song even more of an embarrassment.

Most of the real fans were watching the game on television screens in pubs and clubs throughout England. As a result, the lethal concoction of alcohol and disappointment inevitably led to outbursts of violence on the streets of England. Many towns were subjected to vandalism and drunken brawling as the sheer magnitude of the disappointment hit home. In the West End of London, the drinkers had converged on Trafalgar Square immediately after the end of the game, and within minutes there were clashes between the fans and the police. Shop windows were smashed and German cars were attacked.

The minute England were knocked out of the tournament, this type of behaviour was always going to happen throughout the country,. Had we been knocked out earlier on in the tournament, I believe Euro '96 would have turned into the biggest non-event of all time. As it was, the tournament will be viewed as a success by most people involved in running the game in this country.

From a security point of view, there had been very little trouble. Sure, there was trouble in London before and after the Scotland game, but this was largely kept under control by the police. There was no real trouble in any of the grounds during the games and what goes on outside in the streets cannot be blamed on the FA. In any case, this trouble was nothing compared to what would have happened if the tournament had been held in Europe.

From a football point of view, it would also be classed as a success by most people. However, you have to remember that England didn't win anything at the end of the day. We were crap against Switzerland and lucky against the Scots and the Spanish. Many people in this country seem to prefer brave losers to winners, but not me. Yes, we played superbly against the Dutch, but it was not enough, and in the end the team let down the nation again

Euro '96 was the final turning point as far as terrace culture in this country is concerned. The England games were attended by smiley happy people with their faces painted, all singing in unison to a pop song written by a couple of comedians. Even the Ebgland - Scotland match had none of the vicious passion that is the ultimate trademark of the greatest derby match in the world. Genuine fans from England and Scotland were prevented from attending the games by the authorities who ensured tickets for the games were impossible to come by, unless you happened to work for one of the sponsors. However, our love of the game and terrace culture will never be allowed to die completely and the casuals were still there, all be it drinking in the West End rather than at Wembley.

Families and females were now the main group of people attending the games and we now have to listen to their expert opinions on a game they have only been interested in for five minutes. It sickens me to see people like this at these games when it is the young lads from the housing estates all over England that gave football its working class roots and made the game popular throughout the world. Football is now seen as a trendy pastime, somewhere to be seen at, and something to discuss in the wine bar after work on a Friday night.

Will these new fans have any loyalty when something new comes along? Will they hell. It will be down to the real fans to return to the new plastic seats, in grounds hardly recognisable from those of ten or 20 years ago. Unless your football team or your country is in your blood, the passion and loyalty will never be there and it is this passion that football clubs and the national team need to utilise if they are to survive or become a success. Unfortunately, in the present climate, they do not appear to appreciate this.

Conclusion

THE SCOTLAND MATCH was the last time I watched England play live. I seriously considered going to Rome in 1997 and France in 1998 for the World Cup, but when I looked into the cost and the travel arrangements for the Italy and France trips, I decided I would rather spend my money on more peaceful pursuits.

A few weeks before the Italy game, I returned to Dublin for a weekend on the piss. I had a fantastic time and really appreciated what a good time we could have enjoyed in Dublin's fair city back in 1990 and 1995 if we had not behaved in such an aggressive fashion. Don't get me wrong, I enjoyed my previous trips to Dublin, but on this occasion, I could actually enjoy the hospitality of the Irish people, and the girls in particular, without worrying about mobs of irate locals or even mobs of other English people from other parts of the country. I would much rather spend my hard earned money in this fashion than running riot and watching my back at all times.

Despite this new mature approach to life, I still miss the buzz and excitement that goes hand in hand with being part of the invading army from England. Like many other people, I was down the pub to cheer the boys on against the Italians. The largest cheer of the night obviously greeted the final whistle and our qualification for the World Cup, but when the cameras homed in on the English fans fighting in the ground during the game, the pub roared its approval.

There are many people who disapprove of football violence and I have no qualms with that. However, the reason this type of behaviour was greeted with cheers from drinkers in England was because our boys were protecting themselves from aggressive Italian police, and from what I could see, our boys were showing no fear. Throughout our illustrious history, Englishmen have been brought up to defend themselves. We wouldn't be the rich prosperous country we are now without this fighting spirit. Our forefathers fought in this manner when they were younger, and here, in the twilight of the Twentieth Century, our boys were still fighting against the Romans.

The police eventually gained the upper hand, but not before quite a few of our boys had been injured. Clearly, they had been provoked by mouthy Italian ultras, but as usual the Italian police concentrated their efforts on battering Englishmen. No change there then.

The reaction in the tabloid press over the following weeks indicated a sudden change in their attitude towards the English fans however. There were cries of anger about how English people could be treated in this way and calls for the heavy handed Italian police to be brought to justice for their knee jerk reactions. I found this all rather curious. Sure, the police had reacted in a brutish manner, but this was nothing new. The Italian police have treated English fans like that on practically every occasion England fans have watched a game in Italy. Other police forces, such as the Dutch and the Spanish police have behaved in a similar fashion over the years, but never have they been condemned by the media. Why the change in attitude now then?

It soon became apparent that a few 'important' people had been hurt by the Italian police. Many people had travelled to Rome as part of corporate packages and they had found themselves attacked by the police for no other reason than they were English. The son of David Mellor was at the game, and he too had been frightened by the behaviour of the police. These kind of people had never been to watch England away in the past and therefore had no comprehension of the type of abuse England fans routinely have to suffer.

Most of us are immune to it and accept it as part and parcel of following England, but the corporate hospitality fans weren't prepared to fight back with their fists and were probably grateful for the presence of the so-called hooligans who were willing to defend the English supporters. Instead of fighting, the new breed chose to voice their opinions to the establishment back home. The Government and the media listen to these people, whereas they would never listen to the ordinary fans who had been subject to such abuse.

I suppose it was a good thing really that this issue was brought to the attention of the middle classes in England. Hopefully, it might put them off trying to act like football fans when in reality they are nothing more than middle class rugby fans trying to behave in a laddish way because they think it's the trendy thing to do. Birds, booze and football is the new lad culture, inspired by all the lads magazines now on the market. However, people like this will never be lads simply because they try too hard to behave like the

155

characters in that pathetic programme, *Men Behaving Badly.* The real lads are the ones that have been going to football for years and accept that violence and police brutality is part and parcel of the trip. If the new breed of fans don't like the scary parts of football, they should watch the game on television in their local wine bar and leave the tickets for the real lads who can look after themselves and are prepared to stand and fight for their country.

The hype surrounding the World Cup in France was enormous. As usual, the press offered the usual horror stories about how England fans would not be able to gain access to the ground unless the ticket had your name and address on. There were also stories of how the Argentinians were waiting for the English and would be seeking revenge for the Falklands War. All bullshit as usual. The French authorities ripped off the England fans and made it virtually impossible for most fans to travel over to France and watch England play.

I decided against making the trip, but it came as no surprise to me when I switched on the news the day before our opening game and saw the street battles in Marseilles. If the French authorities had been serious about wishing to prevent trouble, why the hell did they chose to host an England - Tunisia game in the most violent city in France? A city that is populated by thousands of North Africans who regularly riot in the city anyway.

Watching the trouble on television, it was clear that the England fans were coming under attack from the Africans, yet the one sided reporting was a disgrace. The England fans who went to Marseilles deserve a medal not abuse, and earned my respect entirely. They were attacked by the local hooligans then attacked by the police, and many found themselves locked up in a foreign prison. And for what I ask?

Their only crime was to be English and to be proud of the flag of St George. If English journalists think patriotism and bottle are national attributes that we should be ashamed of, then they can think again. Rest assured, we will never change!

Come ahead if you think you're hard enough . . .

Terrace Banter was launched in October, 1998, as a football imprint of S.T. Publishing. Over the past decade football as a spectator sport has changed beyond all recognition, particularly for the ordinary fan. A great deal of working class culture and tradition is being cast to one side so that football can appeal to a new market, that of the "socca fan".

Through Terrace Banter we hope to put down in print the experiences of the ordinary fan before they are lost forever in a sea of plastic seats and replica strips. Unless we document our own history, it is left to outsiders and the mass media to be judge and jury.

We are interested in hearing from other authors who would like to publish a book about their exploits as a football supporter, no matter the team. Each book would represent a piece in a jigsaw puzzle, and together would give as good a picture of what life is like for the ordinary fan as you're likely to find.

Even if you don't think you could write the book yourself, we can help you get your words into print.

You can contact us at

Terrace Banter
S.T. Publishing
P.O. Box 12
Lockerbie
DG11 3BW
Scotland

info@terracebanter.com
www.terracebanter.com